My life
A long and winding road

The Story of a Sinner come to Christ

www.fast-print.net/store.php

A Long And Winding Road

ISBN 978-178035-315-9

All profits from the sale of this account are being donated to the
Panarwar hostel in India to help in the good work they are doing
there with children in need. Please excuse any typo's or spelling
mistakes as professional proof reading costs money, money that
I prefer go to Panarwar.

WARNING. This account contains adult themes, some of which
are of a sexual nature that some readers may find offensive. This
account may also be unsuitable for some younger readers.
Parental discretion is recommended.

First published 2012 by
FASTPRINT PUBLISHING
Peterborough, England.

I dedicate this book to my saviour Jesus and pray that this story will help bring others to His love.

I also thank my wife Christine (Kris), for all her help and support throughout and for her faith and strength when mine was lacking. To the 51st Highlanders without whom I probably wouldn't be here. To Dave and Annie, for their love and faith when they helped a stranger in trouble in a foreign land.

And to all those people who have been kind enough to help, by reading, and by commenting, especially Janet and her red pen.

Chris, January 2012.

Annie and Dave

Contents

The Child

'Before you judge me, try hard to love me, look within your heart then ask, have you seen my childhood'.

Michael Jackson

Foreword

When I first began writing 'My life' I wasn't at all sure where it would go. I knew my life had in a lot of ways been different to most other people, but frankly 'so what?'

I had no wish to parade my mistakes and wrong doings for others to read and judge me by, why would I want to?

Like everyone else I was born and walked a path through life that is in the most part determined by our upbringing and personal circumstances, in other words our parents, our role models, and the society we live in.

One way we learn is by experience, as a child we copy our elders, absorb their views and prejudices. It is only as we get older that we really develop choice, often by then it is too late to change without help, help that sometimes isn't available.

My story is not in itself remarkable, so many people live in circumstances that would make my story seem tame, so many have gone through their lives set in the mould they grew up in, unable or unwilling to change.

So why am I writing it?

I want to show you, the reader, that if you are suffering in your life because of your upbringing or you have been abused or you are now an abuser then don't lose heart you can live a better life. Help is freely available, you only have to ask.

I am not writing a diary here, it sometimes wanders rather than running from A to Z, I make no apology for that, this account is mine, written as I want it to be.

Names have been changed to protect the guilty as well as the innocent; I have no right to judge, and where they were in their life then may not be where they are now, being identified in this would surely hurt some who don't deserve it.

I hope by your reading this you will find it interesting and hopefully of use to you if you want to change your life.

I have been saved, my sins washed away, born anew.

You too can say that, live a better life as I am, it's up to you. It's your choice, to go on as you are, or to 'be born again' as a new person.

Chris Hyde January 2012

My Mother when I was 17yrs

Chapter 1. The Nightmare that was Childhood

In the beginning

There were the heavens and the earth, and I arrived in them at 4.30am on a cold February morning in a small cottage in Llandaff, then a village just outside Cardiff in South Wales. It is now a suburb of Cardiff and my home is a car park.

I was born on the kitchen table, normal practice in those days as it made life easier for both mother and midwife.

A good scrub and a sheet and a pillow were all that was needed.

However my arrival was not to be without incident. As I emerged the midwife tied off the umbilical cord and cut it, and then as she was lifting me to my mother I shot out of her hands like a bar of wet soap and landed on the stone floor of the cottage. Welcome to the world.

In light of how my life was to progress this was perhaps an omen of things to come.

Two hours later my father ate his breakfast at the same table, before leaving for work, prepared I understand by the midwife.

I was upstairs with my mother.

My life had begun.

My parents and 'The War'

My mother was a small dark haired woman, from pictures of her in her Auxiliary Territorial Service (ATS) uniform she looked attractive but not beautiful, like so many women of that era the uniform suited her, my father obviously thought so anyway. This country was again at war (39-45) with everyone 'doing their bit'; he was in the infantry a tall slim man with dark wavy hair and a friendly smile. He was serving with the British Expeditionary Force (BEF) in France during what was later known as the 'phoney war' and then the retreat to and subsequent rescue from Dunkirk of the shattered remains of our army.

I have often looked at this campaign and marvelled at how this stunning series of defeats across France and the subsequent debacle of Dunkirk was turned into the propaganda victory it was by the government of the day. Our army (along with the French) had gone to stop Adolf Hitler and the Third Reich. Germany under the leadership of Adolf Hitler was again threatening peace in Europe, it is argued by some that the First World War never ended as the German army had never been defeated in battle and the period between the wars was only a rearming by all combatants. That the invasion of Poland (The Himmler plan) was merely the continuation of a war that despite the armistice (or perhaps more probably, because of its terms) left Germany feeling hugely aggrieved by the crippling war remunerations it had to pay to the so called 'victors' for a war most Germans felt it had never lost.

It should, I think, be noted that Adolf Hitler served on the western front and received an award for gallantry (Iron Cross 2nd class) so he was among those soldiers who returned to the poverty and unemployment of post-world war one Germany. Undefeated and still well-disciplined they returned to a life of soup kitchens and civil unrest as the population struggled to survive. That a strong right wing party emerged from this cauldron of despair should not have come as a surprise.

Hitler had since his democratic election (something often forgotten) rebuilt Germany, rearmed her and united the population under the Nazi (*Nationalsozialismus*, National Socialism) flag.

I could write all day on this subject but that is not the purpose of this account, I would recommend 'The Two World Wars' by Brigadier Peter Young and Susan Everett as a good starting point for anyone who wants to look a little deeper into this idea than the usual standard of TV documentaries.

At the time France had the largest standing army in Europe and nobody (publicly) had any doubts that we would 'Give them a damm good thrashing and be home for Christmas'. This was not to be however. The German army through a combination of brilliant tactics the 'Manstein plan' (based on a plan previously devised by Von Schlieffen) that utilised Blitzkrieg (lightening war) and superior equipment drove all before it across Europe. Supported by an attack in the Arden region they smashed the French and drove the remains of the British Expeditionary Force (BEF) onto the beaches at Dunkirk and a desperate rescue.

The miracle of Dunkirk (operation Dynamo) as performed by the Royal Navy (who paid dearly losing at least 243 ships sunk, including six Royal Navy destroyers, with another 19 suffering damage). The many ordinary citizens of this country who in pleasure boats and weekend cruisers sailed across to France and literally saved our army is a story of great individual and collective heroism in itself. I shall always be grateful for their courage as my father was one of those rescued from the beaches. My Father had arrived as had so many separated from their units and without any real idea of what was happening, to the chaos of the beach at Dunkirk. It was not the orderly scene sometimes depicted in films more a semi disciplined free for all until control was established. Men were crowding down to the water in desperate haste to find a boat home, later forming lines out as far as they could wade to reach the small boats that were trying to lift them off and deliver them to waiting Royal Navy ships or to head back across the channel overloaded to the point of real danger and home. So many people have a right to say proudly that they risked everything to save those men. Yet it is a story seldom honestly told as propaganda from that era colours accounts even today. The risks those men in small boats took, and the courage of the Royal Navy cannot be over stated. They all played their part in what was after all a heroic but glorious defeat in the true tradition of The Light Brigade at Balaclava (1854).

Bear with me I have to give you some facts here.

British and Allied losses at Dunkirk were very heavy. The BEF lost 68,111 killed, wounded and prisoner, during the retreat across France and the subsequent evacuation. While the RAF lost 106 aircraft during the fighting. The number of prisoners captured is not entirely clear but few estimates go lower than 40,000. People today don't remember the massive losses of that evacuation; we nearly lost our entire army, all of it. Without the commonwealth and the empire this country would have been finished and our history would have been very different.

I must at this point pay tribute to the forgotten heroes of that campaign, the rear guard, ordered to hold 'To the last man or the last round' to keep open the escape route for their comrades. Many paid the ultimate price for this heroic defence. Those that survived that last stand on the cliffs at St Valery en Caux by the 51st Highlanders were to spend the next five years as prisoners and forced labour in Poland. Today a poignant reminder of that day stands on that cliff head.

My father was one of the 300,000 (war office estimate) evacuated from the beaches, he also managed to bring home a souvenir of that time. During one of the strafing attacks by the German air force (the Luftwaffe) he had taken cover with many others in the sand dunes. During one attack he felt a blow on his helmet, when he looked he saw a dent where a shell had creased it but had failed to explode. He dug it out of the sand behind him where he had been and brought it home with him. In later years in Italy he had it made up into a ring that he always wore.

I have written a little more than I intended about Dunkirk but I wanted to show how tenuous had been my father's hold on life at that time and make the point that if that shell had been one inch lower I would never have existed.

I know very little about my father's wartime experiences, like so many others he didn't enjoy talking about those days. I do know he served with the 8th army (the desert rats) in the campaigns against Rommel, then in Italy at the Selerno landings and later at Monte Casino. It was here I think having witnessed so much pointless slaughter at this place that he changed both as a person and as a soldier.

During the winter and spring of 1944 allied forces comprising an assortment of British, American, French, Italian, Polish, Australian, Canadian and North African troops were engaged in attacking the mountain top monastery at Monte Casino, Italy.

With ice cold winds in winter that could freeze a vehicle's engine solid in minutes and baking hot in summer, the mountains and valleys around Casino are an inhospitable area where an estimated quarter of a million men were killed, wounded or missing (presumed killed).

By bombing the monastery that sat atop the mountain (allegedly being used as an observation post by the Germans to overlook the entire valley) the allies had given the defending German army a mass of rubble instead of a building to defend, perfect cover to fight from; this action has often been compared to the battle for Stalingrad in its ferocity and for its cost in lives on both sides. I know that after it my father transferred to the medical core and spent the rest of the war putting himself in even more danger by trying to save the lives of his fallen comrades.

As a child I never realised what a brave man he must have been, or what horror he had witnessed. As a child my favourite comic was 'The Victor' for boys, (stories of WW2, from the British point of view, more propaganda!).

I wonder now what he thought when he saw me reading about the campaigns he had taken part in, what were his feelings then, what were his memories?

I'm not sure when my mother and father married but I think it was about 1946, a church wedding she in white and he in his uniform. All I can remember is one faded photograph showing them outside a church vestibule, they both look happy standing together in the sunshine.

I think it is one of the only occasions I ever remember seeing them look so happy together. In all the other photographs I have seen my father looks somewhat withdrawn as he poses for the camera. In less formal shots I have seen he is grinning with a smile I still remember but seldom saw.

In 1947 my father was demobbed back to 'civvy Street'.

Born of a poor family in Aston (a suburb of Birmingham), one of seven (surviving) children from a terraced row in the back streets my father never had a great deal. Joining the army was a common way out of poverty in the years between the wars when unemployment was rife and there was no socialist state to support those without a job. However now he had to find work, with no qualifications and little schooling he eventually found work in the Welsh steel works at Portalbot where he worked in the press shops making steel for the growing car manufacturing market.

He once showed me a scar on his hand that ran from palm to between his thumb and fingers where a steel sheet had caught him as he worked it. In those day's life in a steel works was dangerous and dirty work that could eventually destroy men. I don't think he enjoyed his time there; certainly he tried to improve himself by improving his literacy skills and learning more mathematics than the very basic skills he had gained at school.

Eventually he brought his family to England to try for a better life, he took and passed the entrance examination and joined the police force in Warwickshire as a police constable, a rank he held for fourteen years.

From this point my father's life and career took a very different path than it would have had he remained a steel worker in Wales. He eventually rose to become (after leaving the police force) 'second in command' to the board of directors of this country's largest private security company, he was in charge of the overall security policies to prevent theft either by robbery of vans or branches or by embezzlement by staff. In this role he excelled, holding the post until his death.

However In 1953 my father was still a PC when my sister arrived and our family was complete.

The early years and school

Home, at first a cottage in Wales what can I really remember? A stone quarry tile floor, red I think. And a window with a tree branch outside, four panes and pale curtains. I have flashes of memory of sitting in a blue high chair with my mother washing the floor, scenes from a time when I was too young to know what I was seeing or to understand it, only to remember flashes of it. I left Wales when I was, I think, about 2 years old.

My mother was beginning to beat me by then, perhaps she always had I don't remember.

At four and a half years old I started school. My life at home seemed normal to me wasn't it the same for everyone? How was I to know anything different? That in fact for most children beatings weren't a common punishment. If something is part of your life then it feels normal and at least to me, at that time it did.

School, I hated it! I began my school life at Nuneaton infant's school. An old Victorian building with iron railings around it that had somehow survived the scrap metal collecting of the war years, and, I regret to say, the bombing.

I remember high ceilings and green and cream painted corridors, racks of hooks with coats and homemade bags for gym kits hung on them, the smell of damp.

There were the cold wet mornings with the inevitable winter smog hanging in the air. I can remember being perhaps five or six years old and my mother slapping me repeatedly around the legs while dragging me by the arm to make me let go of the school railings because I didn't want to go in. Memories of being dragged screaming past those railings stay with me even today.

I was already falling behind the others in my class and becoming a lonely quiet child. What actually started my dislike of school I can't now remember but I think it may have had a lot to do with how I was treated at home. I never really felt part of anything or that I really belonged or was even wanted.

I was to discover in later years that this was probably true and that my mother never really found it easy to love me for reasons that would eventually become clear.

I don't ever remember having friends in those early years, I knew other children and I suppose I ran and played and made a nuisance of myself but no memory of having a friend stays with me from this period of my life.

School for me was becoming the lesser of two evils. I hated school; I was not a good student and was never going to be. I had no friends. The only reason I went was to escape my life at home. Examinations were for me a nightmare, as W. S. Churchill said in his memoirs on the subject of examinations 'the examiners always contrived to ask me what I didn't know rather than what I did'. For me the feeling was that no matter how hard I tried the end result was always the same, failure.

Because of my father's job we moved every few years so I learnt to do without friends without realising it at the time. Each day was just to get through, perhaps dreaming of the day when I could leave it all behind me.

I was a quiet introverted child preferring to stay in and read rather than go outside, what was the point who could I play with? As I grew I think I realised that somehow I was different, that in some way I was apart from the other children of my age group. I was always uncomfortable with other children; I wonder now how many others felt the same, how many others were hiding bruises under school trousers and rolled down shirt sleeves. Were they also afraid to show anyone, afraid to let others know how naughty they must be.

How many like me were afraid to go home never knowing what was waiting there. These are questions with no answers. Certainly I was not the only one, but I was alone in myself, as were they, so it was just part of life to me, unpleasant, painful but normal.

Over the years between infants and junior school I remember so many times coming home to find my mother in a raging temper over something, and inevitably within minutes I had apparently done something that required her to punish me. How often that happened I can't guess but I remember some of it with the clarity of yesterday. How often did I go to bed crying and confused sore and hungry, hate inside me beginning to find a focus?

I often wondered why my father did nothing to stop those beatings; he was hardly incapable of doing so but never did.

Perhaps because he was at work, so often working shifts or asleep he didn't see it as a problem or maybe he just didn't want to see it. My mother could be a very loud abusive person, so perhaps he just wanted a little peace and couldn't handle her temper tantrums either. Maybe he was afraid of her.

Whatever the reason, I soon learnt that he wasn't going to help me.

For many years I felt a deep resentment over this apparent attitude of disinterest in my situation but in a strange way I can now understand him. I too have turned a blind eye to things to keep the peace in a relationship and I don't honestly think he really knew how bad it got at times for me. Or how bad it must have been for him, in those days to leave and divorce while in the police force would not have been looked upon with understanding by his superiors. And there was another reason that at this time I did not even suspect or had considered, it would be years before I knew the truth and perhaps began to understand him more fully.

By eight or nine I had learnt to take the beatings, crying or yelling did no good so I learnt to take it and be silent in my pain. This gave me some pleasure as at least I was not going to give her (my mother) the satisfaction of hearing me cry. This of course led to the beatings increasing in their severity but I would not give in and remained silent and defiant, learning to hide my pain and my emotions.

A lot of my earliest memories are of violence, beatings for saying or doing the wrong thing, my injuries at the hospital – he fell, he tripped on the stairs. I was too frightened to say anything different.

This started as a toddler and went on until I was big enough to prevent it. I was probably one of the first children into long trousers for school to cover the bruises. I didn't do games and what was then called physical training, partly because of my health. I was always underweight for my age and prone to colds and various childhood ailments.

The many occasions when I had been sent to bed without anything to eat must also have played a part in my appearance.

When I was about eight or nine I had the only birthday party I can remember, I know after that one I never had or wanted another. It was a sunny February day. It must have been the weekend as I had been allowed to 'play out', a rare treat for me as I was mostly kept close to the house usually in the back garden, but on this occasion I remember coming home to change ready for 'my party 'that afternoon.

There were maybe six or seven other children coming among them the first love of my life Karen B. Blond, blue eyes and also a loner, maybe she had similar problems to me at home because she often seemed reluctant to go straight home from school. In the years following this occasion I have often wondered what became of her. I lost track I can't remember if she moved away or I did. Whenever I do think of her I wonder if she like me suffered when the front door closed behind her and witnesses were excluded.

Well finally the time arrived and we all played the usual games. For me then it was the happiest I can ever remember being. For a few brief hours I was part of the group, probably because it was my party but accepted none the less.

Then it happened, disaster I dropped a glass of pop onto the floor and it smashed spilling the pop across the wooden floor some going onto the carpet. Well my mother went mad, the carpet was ruined – why had I done it, why had I been so naughty, I can't remember my answers, why does a child drop anything? It just happens doesn't it, no, not according to my mother. According to her nothing was ever an accident it was usually a sign of disobedience and must therefore be punished.

So in front of everyone there and then I had my pants pulled down and was given 'a good spanking for my own good' after which everyone was sent home and I was sent to bed, probably for my own good as well. How long does it take for a child to learn to hate? I know that my feelings for my mother never included love, only distrust and confusion, why was I the only one treated this way?

I can still remember the shame of the days following that party, were people pointing me out, I don't know but I felt like an outcast. I was alone again.

This incident and others like it over the years must have had a lot to do with my wanting to be alone, certainly until the last couple of years at school I had no friends or anyone I was willing to trust. I had already learned not to trust or to show emotion, if nobody knows you are crying inside then they can't jeer or mock you. Don't trust, don't show what you are feeling and never let anyone get close enough to be able to hurt you. Those became my rules for life and my way of surviving.

The years at school passed as they do for all children, some good some bad. I had become a reader, never without a book or two in my bag. In books I felt safe (I still do). I could go anywhere, do anything. Reality was banished for a while by H. G. Wells, Enid Blyton and Daniel Defoe. The popular children's comics never interested me, they were full of make believe characters. 'Biffo the bear' or 'Mini the minx' left me unmoved.

A book was a way out of the life I was trapped in. I read Robinson Crusoe and the picture of that island has stayed with me all my life. My dream world born of a desire to be anywhere but where I actually was, somewhere I could escape to. HG Wells when he wrote 'The Time Machine' contributed in no small measure to the love of physics I have developed and enjoyed all my life. I enjoy science fiction not fantasy. The work must have some possible basis in reality and not in magic, I suppose it was the same for comics they had no basis in reality either.

We moved around a lot in those days. Every four or five years it was a new school and a new start.

In some ways it helped. I was unknown again but being the son of a local police officer and a new boy and introvert usually meant that the first year was made hell for me by the school bullies.

Why didn't I fight back? Well there are several answers to that question. Between four and thirteen I had bronchitis and pneumonia and my kidneys failed. I also had of course all the usual childhood ailments chicken pox and coughs and colds including the 'accidents' I had at home that left me bruised and stiff. All in all, until I was in my teens I was small and light for my age. I had also become used to being hit, it seemed just part of life, the way things were.

It all seemed so normal, how was I to know that for most children going home to their family was a joyful thing full of happiness, a loving family. To me it meant trying every moment not to anger my mother, trying to put off the inevitable beating that would come for the most trivial of mistakes.

I have to make it clear that I am not talking about 'a slap' or a clip around the ear. I am talking about being pulled over my mother's lap and being hit repeatedly until she felt I had learned my lesson. Sometimes this meant three or four blows at other times it could mean many more. If I made the mistake of trying to get away, that always led to a more severe beating, not just my bottom but arms legs, head any part of me she could reach. These beatings were accompanied by her shouting and swearing at me as she hit me and would go on until she was exhausted and walked away sending me to my room to 'get out of her sight'. I still carry a small scar from one of those beatings where I was thrown across the room and fell into the open and lit fire; luckily I landed on the fender and rolled away screaming. No doubt that was my fault as well.

I remember these beatings with a clarity that even now makes my skin crawl. To this day I have problems with claustrophobia, nothing really bad. If I keep control of my fear then I can cope with it.

I came home one day to my mother in 'a mood'. I don't remember the reason now but the result was I had done something wrong again and had to be punished. I was beaten, then stripped and locked in the larder. I was left there for the next five or six hours. It was cold and dark, at some point my mother went out and I was alone in the house. I was finally let out and sent to bed just before my father was due home, probably about ten thirty at night. I will never forget sitting on that stone floor in the dark and the fear of that place, the shame that I had wet myself, the damp concrete floor, naked and so fearful of what may yet happen. Crying and wondering why nobody would help me.

I suppose some people realised what was going on at home but nobody did anything. I came from what today would be termed an abusive background however in the 1950's people took less notice of what went on behind closed doors.

At about this time we were living in Sutton Coldfield just outside Birmingham and I was a thin scrawny child of twelve years with few friends, beginning to get into trouble. Windows got smashed, cars had scratches on them, and other small stuff but a trend was developing.

I was also learning that if you weren't caught then you didn't do it.

Truth was what someone could prove, not what actually happened. My mother had taught me that.

I was a loner; trust meant someone else knowing what really happened or how you really felt. Then they had a power over you or could betray you for their own ends.

Not that I was bothered by that fact by now I was learning to be self-reliant and never to trust anyone. For that same reason I never kept a diary until later in life and then only for business use.

A revelation and an explanation

It was about this time that I learned two more lessons, the first about women's 'periods,' the menstrual cycle, and the second, why my mother apparently never loved or wanted me. In the space of a few days my feelings for my mother and the course of my life would be changed forever by two incidents.

Life at home had never been good, but now for reasons I don't remember, or perhaps never knew, it had become a lot worse.

My parents were arguing it seemed every day. They were shouting at each other, hurling abuse back and forth, somehow forgetting, or not caring that Lyn and I were there in the house hearing it all. Things got smashed or just disappeared from sight (presumably thrown away), doors had to be repaired or repainted. I was walking on egg shells afraid of saying or doing the wrong thing. I was so afraid of triggering yet another outburst from my mother, and receiving another beating. Every time I came home from school I knew I was risking that beating. Looking back now I still believe as I did then that there was a 'tension' in the air between my parents that was far above the normal day to day stress of our family life. The beatings had increased over the weeks both in their severity and frequency to the point where my mother had actually broken a wooden toilet brush while beating me with it while I was in the bath. That particular beating resulted in a trip to hospital the next day because my left arm and my face were so swollen and bruised. I had no doubt 'fallen' again. In any case nothing was broken so I was sent home.

I thank God that these days a child in this situation has more chance than I had of some action being taken on their behalf. Even so many cases of abuse go unreported and many children still suffer behind closed doors at the hands of abusive parents.

I didn't need to do anything to be punished; just being there was reason enough. The safest course of action was to get to our bedroom as soon as we got home from school (Lyn and I shared a room) as quickly as possible. If we were called for tea, fine, if not it was safer not to ask, better to go hungry than risk upsetting my mother and lighting that fuse which inevitably burned towards an explosion of temper and violence.

It was during one of the now frequent arguments between my mother and father that I was to witness what for me at the time was what I believed mistakenly, was the violent assault of my mother by my father.

They were shouting at each other, perhaps screaming would be a better description, in the hall. My sister and I were in the kitchen 'keeping out of the way' when we heard a crash and a scream and the sound of something landing hard on the stairs.

I rushed into the hall to see my mother lying back on the stairs with my father standing over her.

Her face was contorted and full of hate as she looked at my father. It was a look I knew well for I had seen it many times as she beat me. I was terrified and wanted to turn and run. This was the only time however that I remember seeing her look this way at my father. She saw me and reached under her dress and lifted her hand out screaming that she was bleeding and 'he' (my father) had done it.

Horrified and scared by what I had seen I ran from the house yelling and screaming, it was only being caught by my father in the street that stopped me going for help. I was screaming and crying hysterically, it was as if something in me had finally cracked and all the fear and despair was coming out at once. It took him a long time to calm me down to the point that he could talk and explain what I had seen. He sat with me in my bedroom holding me and trying to calm me until finally I could listen to what he had to say.

Yes he had pushed my mother away from him to prevent her hitting him but that was all. It seems that I was not the only one who had to bear her assaults. How often she had done that to my father I can only guess but it was evident from what I learnt later that it was not uncommon behaviour on her part.

She was a nasty violent woman who seemed to have no love in her.

That's how I learnt about the menstrual cycle; my father had to explain to his twelve year old son after he had been through that experience, what it was really all about. Afterwards I understood the process but I have never forgotten the horror of that experience.

For months I had nightmares far too graphic to describe here about what I had seen. Occasionally I still do. Parents, think what you do with your children. Don't give them my memories, or my nightmares.

Up to this time I had no idea about the menstrual cycle other than a vague idea that women had 'their troubles' once a month. I know that this must sound odd but I was twelve and my sister ten or maybe just eleven. In our house such things were never talked about because as I learned later my mother thought it was a 'dirty' subject. My mother had been taught by her mother that it was a curse from God because Eve had led Adam astray. My grandmother was firmly Welsh Chapel, no dancing or singing other than hymns. Sex was to be borne and was only for having children and not for enjoyment. After the experience I had been through it would be years before I could talk about 'periods' without feeling I was being somehow 'dirty'. My sister found out about it when she started her first period, she was thirteen.

She was in a gym class and the teacher noted a fresh stain on her shorts. The teacher must have been shocked when my sister screamed in fear. She thought she was hurt. It was left to the school nurse to explain the truth and how to deal with it. How awful it must have been for Lyn to have that happen in front of her class mates.

I don't remember much of what happened in the months after that but I know I still have a picture in my head even after all these years of that scene on the stairs. What she was thinking I can only guess but if any day finally sealed my feelings for my mother then it was that day.

Hate and distrust from then on, until I could escape were all I now felt for her. I couldn't understand or even begin to describe all my feelings but any love I still felt for her had died there that day never to return.

This was just one incident, granted it was one of the more extreme but in a lot of ways it was typical of my mother's behaviour. She never considered the consequences of her actions, the phrase 'I didn't mean it I was angry' was the usual response after the event. To this day I find it almost impossible to listen to this and to forgive. Had she been believed it might have cost my father his job or at the very least it would have been investigated by the police, his colleagues.

He told me years later that for him that day was also the end. Had he not been brought up to believe that he had a responsibility to his family no matter what; he may have left and made a new life for himself somewhere else?

Considering what was to come for him, what his future held, I find it difficult not to believe that he should have left then. At least he would have had a chance of happiness. However for us, his children he stayed.

I would never trust a woman again for forty five years because of this and the many other incidents in my childhood believing all women to be liars and never to be trusted.

How often did my mother tell me (and Lyn) that she was dying and we would be sorry when she was gone? How often did she threaten me that if I told anyone any of my 'lies' about what happened at home I wouldn't wake up one day? That she would smother me in the night with a pillow if I disobeyed her. I can still see her face close to mine as she described what she would do to me. Claustrophobia and the vision of that pillow still haunt me in my nightmares fifty years later.

It's hard to explain the atmosphere in our house over the next few days.

I was having nightmares and not eating, my arm and face still very bruised, I had lost one tooth. I was afraid to even look at my mother. My father completely ignored her, they 'weren't speaking'; my sister just seemed to be able to keep out of the way of my mother as usual either by going out or staying in our bedroom.

It was a few days later, I was still off school because of my bruising when my mother turned on me. My father had gone to work after another argument between them and I was alone in the house with her I don't remember where my sister was, probably at school.

What I had done I can't remember. We were in the kitchen. I remember she was washing up and I was sitting at the kitchen table. She turned and hurled a pile of plates from the table to the floor and screaming at me that I 'was never the son she wanted' but 'he had died' and what she got was me. I fled from the room and hid in my bedroom expecting the door to be flung open at any moment by my mother in a rage. Then would come the inevitable beating, on this occasion however she left me alone.

This was the first time I had ever been told this and it bothered me greatly.

Normally I had learned to ignore all she said and treat it as nothing more that the ravings of a sick mind, a conclusion I had held for some years based on what little I knew of 'madness' gained from horror films or TV programs. In my young mind the ravings of the lunatics in Hammer horror stories were not so dissimilar to my mother's ravings. This however had a ring of truth about it. What had she meant?

Like all children (am I right here?) I had fantasised about being adopted. Certainly Lyn and I had talked about not really belonging to the parents we had and this was my first thought. Was I right after all these years? Was this the truth, I really was adopted? That I had loving parents out there somewhere who would come and save me? It would explain so much. I think it also shows how naive and desperate I was at the time to believe that the parents who had put me up for adoption would come like some avenging angels to save me, realise their mistake and take me home with them to live happily ever after.

For days this ran through my mind. Where had I come from, where did I really belong?

Who was my real mother or in fact who were my real parents?

The nightmares I was still having and this thought were tearing me to pieces inside. I had to know the truth. There was only one person I trusted enough to ask.

Finally, I did what in a way I had been dreading doing, because despite my mother and the unhappiness of my home life I loved my father greatly and respected him, so I asked him for the truth, was I adopted?

His reaction was almost a confirmation to me and I still remember the feeling as my stomach sank; he looked at me and said quietly 'we have to talk, let's go outside'. We went into the garden and sat on a low wall. It's another of the scenes that still live with me. My father sitting next to me, looking so worried, yet so compassionate. He then gently told me the story of my brother, a brother I had never heard of or suspected had ever existed.

He had been born the year before me a few weeks premature but healthy and from all accounts without any obvious 'defects', but there was something wrong. As the hours passed he grew weaker and finally died about 36 hours after his birth.

My parents had lost their first son.

My father came to terms with it but I don't think my mother ever did and that may go a long way to explaining her treatment of me.

Of course I could never be the son she wanted and it wasn't until then that I began to understand why. Did that change how I felt about her? I was too young to be able to reason as an adult might, for me then it was just more proof that I had never been loved or wanted by her, that I was a replacement that had failed to measure up to the son she had lost. I don't know his name, did he have a name? I don't know, to me he will always be my big brother and for that he doesn't need a name.

Time went on and things settled down again. I don't remember any more hospital trips. I still got beatings, these would continue for some years yet until I finally stopped them, but that comes later.

I do think of him sometimes and wonder how different so many lives would have been had he lived. How would I have grown up having a 'big brother'? What would it have done for the way I treated women in my own life later? How much pain might have been saved had he only lived? With his dying the lives of so many were changed in ways that could never have been foreseen by mortal man.

That year shaped my attitudes, my beliefs, even laid the foundations for my mental illness that was to come and for the violent behaviour that would be with me for most of my life.

I have said 'If I could go back and change anything then it would be that year' but to be completely honest I think I would be afraid to, who knows what the alternative might have been? Who would I now be? Who knows why these things happen, only God, and his plan is far beyond my puny understanding.

The final move

I was by now thirteen, almost fourteen years old and beginning to want some of the things I saw that others of my age had, a bike, a pair of binoculars for watching animals in the wild, I was developing a love of the outdoors and survivalist skills, and of course later, parts for the various models I made.

My main income came from a paper round, I was very lucky because my round included the local barracks of the Welsh guards The Royal Welsh Fusiliers who were, like all squaddies, generous to me as a kid when paying for their papers and would often give me the change. Over a week I probably made more from these tips than from my regular wage.

I had developed an interest in aircraft and would spend many hours looking at pictures or reading about the history behind a particular aeroplane.

I was particularly interested in aircraft of the First World War. It fascinated me to think that man had gone from flying a few short miles to full air combat in that period. I learnt about lift, drag and power to weight ratios, in other words how an aircraft flies. But, more importantly, as Wilber and Orville Wright discovered how to control that flight was the challenge. With big enough engines a brick can be made to fly but controlling that flight requires an understanding of aerodynamics. This in time led to building models and at one time I had a regular world air force hanging from my bedroom ceiling, mostly first and Second World War combat aircraft but also a fair selection of civil aircraft of the era. Usually the more eccentric aircraft were featured, multi winged or just simply huge like the Handley Page bomber of 1915 a twin engine biplane and the later 1918 V1500 that was still a bi-plane but it boasted four engines.

These early aircraft still fascinate me and may become another hobby when I retire, I have to admit the thought of a fully radio controlled 30" wingspan four engine V1500 does appeal.

Because of my father's work and the regular moves I never felt as though we (the family) really belonged, consequently my schooling suffered as did the ability to form lasting friendships. Although to be fair I never really missed not having friends, I was even at that age fairly self-sufficient.

Around this time my father left the police force still as a PC having taken and failed the exam for sergeant again. His poor literacy and numeracy skills let him down again and again, despite his efforts to improve himself. I suppose he became disillusioned with going nowhere in the police service so he applied for a job with a security company as a van guard. It meant we had to move again but this time it would be out of the Midlands and down to the South West of England.

As it turned out this was to be another change in his life, he took the job and by virtue of his ability and hard work was promoted steadily.

I remember well how proud he was when he was finally promoted to assistant to the board of directors some years later, he had worked hard and had at last been rewarded.

I should clarify at this point that my father was a very gentle man. Physically he was a big man, fit and strong an ex steel worker, quietly spoken with a sense of what was right and wrong about him, he would always listen to me and on occasion covered for me. As a young man I once came home very late and very drunk from a 'staff' night out while working for Curry's. He found me as he was leaving for work the next morning asleep under the hall carpet with my clothes draped over the banister rail I was convinced that I had made it to bed. He quietly woke me and suggested I get to bed before my mother saw me. He never referred to the incident keeping it as our secret.

In all the years he only ever hit me once. I had been particularly obnoxious and said something that must have upset him greatly; he slapped me across the face and sent me to my room. Five minutes later he came up sat on the bed looked at me and apologised for hitting me. That was my father, a gentle giant. I loved him greatly and miss him to this day.

By now the family had settled in Weston Super Mare, relocating for my father's new job. For me this was to be the final move with the family. I was now fourteen years old and I had made a friend, Jim, who probably for the first time in my life was someone I felt I could trust. His problems although different from my own, had left him, too, a loner.

His father had passed away when he was seven or eight leaving his mother to bring up two children alone on a very limited income.

We quickly discovered we shared a love of model aircraft building and then flying them in the local park, by combining our skills and the many spare parts we both had we could achieve so much more.

What was then called 'control line flying' was our main love where the aircraft is controlled by two lines to a handle and flies around you in a fixed circle. You have control of the elevators from your handle, all very exciting for a fourteen year old boy. Taking off, landing or swooping around in loops during simulated combat. The two of us would fly with four or five feet of paper streamers attached to our aircraft both within the same circle standing back to back. The object of this simulated combat being to cut the other's streamer without having one's own cut away. Or for that matter crashing into the ground.

We also made 'free flight' models, aircraft that literally were flown 'free', usually to circle in the sky at about one or two hundred feet until the fuel for the small petrol engines ran out when the aircraft would descend and land to be retrieved by us.

This required considerable skill to set the rudder and ailerons correctly before the flight or the model could either fly out of sight or crash after only a few moments of flight.

On one memorable occasion we launched a solid fuel jet powered glider we had built from the beach at Weston Super Mare, in an attempt to fly it to Wales. A project we had approached with all the seriousness of NASA, calculating lift, fuel loads, flight duration. We launched it and watched it gain height as it headed out to sea over the Bristol Channel. We saw the solid fuel booster drop away as it was exhausted. We watched until it disappeared from sight, still flying on a true course towards the Welsh shores. It was fascinating to us to speculate where it had landed. We had calculated from the approximate height reached when the motor shut down and it became a true glider that it would definitely make the shore. In fact we were convinced it would go some miles inland before landing. We had done several test flights 'free' before this attempt so knew the approximate glide time after engine exhaustion. We had waited until the wind was in our favour. The sun had warmed the land long enough to provide updrafts. However, despite all our plans and preparations, and having our names and addresses inside including a request to contact us by whoever found it we never learned its fate.

Writing this has even today made me sit and wonder what really did happen to it. It should have reached the heavily populated welsh shore. Was it found and the finder couldn't be bothered to contact us in case we wanted it back, or did it end its flight in the cold waters of the Bristol Channel. I will never know but I still wonder, thinking about those unseen final moments in its short life.

Our other great love was explosives. My mother's brass cannon an early victim of our chemical experiments. Brass does not contain an explosion well; the ball bearing we had used as shot left the barrel and buried itself in a close-by tree trunk accompanied by a great cloud of smoke and flame from our home brewed gunpowder, wonderful!

However the barrel was split open from end to end, panic, what could we do? In the end I had to admit to a modified version of what happened to my mother, we were playing with it and lost it. By then I had learned to survive so I waited until my father was home and it was morning, experience had taught me this combination of circumstances seemed to be the least likely to cause my mother to explode and therefore limited the beating in its severity.

We had to pay to replace it, I can't remember how much but all things considered I got off lightly. Those times with Jim were for me the best years of my childhood. He and I were true friends; no matter what the world did we had each other for support.

This was the first time in my life I had ever had a confidant, almost a brother.

To pay for the things I wanted I had taken an after school job delivering groceries for a small local shop. It was at the top of the hill between Weston Super Mare and a place called Sandy Bay.

I had to use one of the heaviest bicycles I have ever seen. It was built like a tank and had baskets both front and rear made of heavy gauge steel. The brakes were a joke and any hills were impossible to climb without getting off and pushing as the gearing was fixed and designed for the flat. Descending was a nightmare of burning rubber brakes and straining on the pedals to slow it as I tried not to let it drop and spill the groceries. All in all a black painted monster that I did combat with every time I rode it.

The only thing I can say in its favour was by the time I left that job I was an awful lot fitter!

The owner, Fred, was a short tubby man who had a habit of touching me around the genitals area when we were passing in the store room. At first just a flick of the fingers as if by accident but as the weeks passed he became more adventurous. I didn't know what to do, it's so easy to look back and make all the right choices but at the time I was frightened of what he might do if I objected and what people would say. Who would they believe and I suppose I didn't want to lose my job.

He would show me pornographic magazines with naked women in and ask me if I masturbated, how it felt, had anyone ever 'helped' me. He once said he had to pee urgently. We were working in the back storeroom together. He positioned himself so I could see what he was doing and urinated into an open drain. I should have left then, but as I said it is easy to make the right choices in hind sight.

He continued in this way until some weeks later. He had me trapped in the store room after he had closed for the day. I was finished with my deliveries and about to go home. I still feel shame at what happened next.

Looking back I now realise that if I had come from a more loving and understanding environment none of this would have happened. I would not have been afraid to tell someone, not afraid to say those words to my parents, to ask for help. However I didn't, so despite my fear or perhaps because of it, I allowed him to unzip me. I was very scared and I knew what he was doing was very wrong but in a strange way excited by the whole thing. What followed would today be described as a sexual assault. I was very scared and ashamed by what had occurred, but until now I have never told anyone about it, not even Jim. I never went back, not even to collect the pay he owed me.

I know now that I should have told either my father or the police but to a boy of my age and upbringing it was so very difficult in those days. It would not have been treated as carefully as it would be now with our child protection laws. I didn't want all the world knowing what had happened. It must also be understood that there was a measure of perceived guilt on my part, what had I done to make this happen? Today when these or similar cases occur it is not unusual for the victim to feel in some way responsible. Of course they aren't but they still feel it. Because of that perceived guilt I believe many abusers still go unpunished and the abused untreated until they seek help in later life when they can better understand what was done to them.

This was a hugely traumatic incident for me that has coloured my attitude towards sex offenders for life. And, re-enforced my growing belief that it was best never to trust anyone, and then you can't be hurt. Making friends became even harder, who can you actually trust? It felt to me then that it was best never to trust fully, always keep the real you safe behind a protective barrier. Anyone who tried to get close to me from then on was met with suspicion and mistrust. Because of this incident it is perhaps the only crime that even today I cannot forgive. There is within me a deep hatred for paedophiles.

Years later, I actually felt proud to be part of a group of men, who, having learned that a convicted paedophile had moved onto 'our' estate went one night, as a mob, and smashed his windows. We stood there hurling abuse and rocks at him, screaming our hate. He had been seen talking to a few of the toddlers on the estate and offering them sweets. That for us and for the mothers of those children was reason enough to drive him out. The hatred I felt at that time for this man cannot be described here; suffice it to say that I had absolutely no sympathy for him.

The police arrived and took him into 'protective custody'. He never came back. Looking back now I am ashamed of my behaviour then, the way I judged him, but even so part of me feels justified because of his crimes against children. I am left with very complex feelings on the subject.

I have never been prejudiced against anyone in my life for their colour, sex, religious beliefs or sexual orientation. Paedophilia is to me different. It is a crime against the truly innocent, against children. When I think of that night, or I see the faces from mob scenes in documentaries I am ashamed that I was part of such a mob, but yet in a way I still feel it was justified. As I said, that incident with Fred has left very complex feelings. One way or another Fred has a lot to answer for. I pray though that he found salvation before he died, and that one day I can truly forgive him for what he did that day.

Jim and I both attended the same school. For our own reasons, we had both ended up in what then was termed the C stream.

Neither of us was badly behaved, just too far behind when it came to exams to have any chance of success.

This was not a big deal to either of us as we had become used to the lack of any chance of academic achievement and were only waiting for that day to come when it would be over and we would be free.

My sister had always been treated differently by my mother and had done well at school, however we were never close and never would be, she escaped punishment by either blaming me or swearing it was not her and being believed.

I don't blame her I would probably have done the same at that age to avoid being hit had I been able to.

It did however leave her with a very pliable personality. She became a 'fence sitter' on any subject, never holding an opinion of her own, that way of course she could never be wrong or to blame.

For many years we did not contact each other until in fact, she was legally required to. Then it was kept to be at a minimum. I am not complaining, I have long forgiven her and do understand why she did what she did but she is not the type of person I would want as a friend and so have never continued contact with her or her family.

There is one blessing to the way Lyn was treated. She and her children have got off the 'roundabout.' She was never beaten as I was so God willing she will not follow the usual route of the abused becoming the abuser.

I left school two weeks before the end of term and as I have said many times since that was the happiest day of my school life. The one finger wave never felt so good.

The only thing I did miss about school was being out most days. Now I was around the house and my mother. Now that is what I call an incentive to find work!

As I remember Jim left the next week, he couldn't wait either.

I gained two things from school however, a love of reading that gave me an escape route, in a book I could be anywhere, do anything, and a lifelong interest in science, physics in particular. The two combined meant that I read an awful lot of science fiction, I still do. Now however I have even started to write some, I have found it is far more difficult than it seemed at first but I am persevering!

A young man of 17 years, just before I joined the Royal Air Force. By now violence was becoming a way of life, I had learnt that to survive you have to be as tough as your abuser, the only way out was through violence overcoming violence.

Chapter 2. Don't Be A Tail Gunner

After school

After gaining my freedom I went to work for Curry's. As a junior salesman the job was mostly cleaning the stock and sweeping the shop, I hated it. One aspect of my job was re-stocking the shop displays. On this particular day I was unpacking washing machines and this was to be one of the many times in my life that my sense of humour nearly got me into trouble. When you unpack a washing machine, first, off comes the cardboard 'box' cover. Then the various polystyrene corners fitted to protect the machine in transit. You are now left with the machine in a close fitting plastic bag. Now for the fun, I moved the machine to the display and put it where it should go, only not quite, I left it annoyingly protruding, at an odd angle. A couple of things to note here, the floor was plastic tile and the washing machine wheels are also plastic, both good electrical insulators. Now, gripping the plastic bag I firmly pulled it off the washing machine as smoothly as possible; then walked away. If you are lucky another assistant will walk past, note the misplaced display and attempt to straighten it. At this point the huge static electric charge you induced when you pulled off the plastic cover discharges through them, screams and swearing usually follows.
Unfortunately I set the 'joke' up only to have a small child touch it first, screams and crying, apologies from the manager, 'can't understand what happened', 'no it is not plugged in', 'so sorry'. Maybe you are reading this and remember that day, if so then may I say a belated sorry for giving you a washing machine phobia for the rest of your life! And no, I never admitted it but most of the shop floor staff knew it was me! I was the butt of many such 'jokes' for some time because of that!

The best part of the job was that I occasionally went out on deliveries or to assist the engineer repairing things in people's homes. I still remember the fascination of degaussing an early colour television for the first time. It seemed like magic to me and fed my growing love of electrical engineering.

I was out one day with the van delivering, I don't remember the make of van but it had sliding doors that would latch open in the hot weather.

Well on this particular day we had the doors open as we drove from delivery to delivery, finally we arrived at the last address where we were delivering a cylinder vacuum cleaner, and I went to the back to pass it out only to find it missing. We both looked stupidly at an empty van and at each other, maybe we hadn't loaded it? After the inevitable shrug we headed back to the shop. Meanwhile, back at the shop, our manager was receiving a telephone call.

An old gentleman had been working in his front garden when we in our van went by. As he lived on a bend in a fairly twisty country lane he didn't get much of a look at us, he did however see the cylinder vacuum cleaner as it shot down his path and landed at his front door.

It seems that the vacuum cleaner had launched itself like a torpedo from the side door and into this chap's garden. Quite a shot really as it passed cleanly through his gate and ran up his path. No damage done but he had got quite a surprise!

Needless to say our manager didn't see the funny side of it, but it was all I could do to keep a straight face when we collected it. The funny thing is I still remember the old chap's face as he told us about it. I swear he was delighted by the whole episode.

I enjoyed those trips out where we could be going a few miles or maybe gone the whole day, it was by far the best part of the job.

Most of my very small wage went on board, the rest, what few pounds I was allowed to keep; I used to buy on a credit sale a Honda 90 motor cycle. I realised that if I used credit then no matter what happened my mother would never risk 'the shame' of debt collectors calling. With my training from Curry's I knew this wasn't the way things worked but it suited me that she thought this.

I paid off the credit within the year and was able to say 'this is mine, nobody else's, its mine'. That was important to me, now, at last, I was becoming independent and the bike gave me a measure of freedom I had never known before.

Jim was also working so he bought a Suzuki 90 motor cycle at about the same time, or perhaps just before I bought mine, I can't really remember.

Jim and I learned to ride these motorcycles together and for the first time I experienced the feeling of complete freedom that riding gave me. To be able to put all my problems, pain and suffering completely out of mind and just feel the pure joy that riding gave me is a feeling that has stayed with me all my life.

I still love to just ride without a fixed destination; there is a sense of freedom and adventure about it, never knowing where the road will lead. In later life this love would lead me to ride across a continent.

I was sacked from that job for theft.

I won't try to justify it but I was young and didn't believe I would ever be caught. I just sometimes 'forgot' to put some of the money from sales of smaller stock, batteries and the like, in the till. Not a lot just a few pounds a week to boost my wages a little, for the 40 hour week as a 'junior salesman' I earned £5-£6 so an extra £1 or £2 made a real difference.

I had been doing it for months when I was caught by an investigation team who came in and did sample purchases that were then checked against the till roll after closing. Caught! Interviewed, dismissed all in one afternoon!

My world fell apart, I couldn't believe it, and I was so ashamed of what I had done or was it of being caught? I had to tell my father the ex-police officer that his son was a thief.

He took it well but I know that I had hurt him deeply. To his great credit he sat with me and we talked about why I had done it, not in the sense of being interrogated but to try and help me understand that whatever the motive I had to take responsibility for my actions. He would be there for me and help all he could but in the end it was up to me. Did I learn from it or continue down that road that he had seen so many young men go down during his time as a PC, the choice was mine. It must have been so hard for him.

I rapidly discovered when I applied for subsequent jobs how important a reference was and how damaging a bad one could be.

Another lesson learned.

I worked for a while for a company that preserved specimens for universities. My job was to remove dog fish we now call them 'rock salmon' from a tank of formaldehyde where they had spent some time soaking up the preservative. I then slid them into a plastic bag ready to be sent out to be dissected by students who, no doubt, never gave a single thought to the person who packed them and because of his job and subsequent body odour never got a date! Needless to say I didn't stay long as a 'packer'.

Various other dead end jobs followed, jobs that held no interest for me other than I was working and earning money.

It was during this period that my mother assaulted me for the last time. I can't remember the exact circumstances, or what I had done. My mother had come at me again swinging her hands and fists. Screaming in rage because I had dodged out of her path she tried to grab me. This time however I was not to be the victim. I wrapped my arms around her, picked her up and threw her into an arm chair. As she tried to rise I put my face in hers, gripped her by the throat and told her that, if she ever laid a hand on me again I would 'beat her f#cking senseless'. Then I went out. I don't remember where, I needed to cool down. For the first time in my life I had let the rage inside me out. It had scared me but it had also scared my mother. This was the beginning of my use of violence to solve my problems. This was the beginning of the behaviour that would shape my life. She never tried to hit me again. If she threatened to I could sense it was an act. All I had to do was look at her. The days of being a victim were, for me, I thought over. I was of course wrong. Until I found Jesus I was now destined to always be a victim of my upbringing, and of my childhood experiences. I didn't know it then of course but Satan had his hand on me, I was becoming one of his.

I was seventeen years old.

The end of a friendship

Jim my only friend and confidant, was killed that year. Murdered, knifed and left to die curled up in some shrubbery behind the Winter Gardens, Weston Super Mare just after his 17th birthday. The medics said he had bled to death slowly overnight.

This was in that period when mods and rockers fought for supremacy over which rode the best machines or had the best lifestyle. We were both in our young minds definitely rockers having motorcycles and all the leathers to fit the image.

After Jim's death I spent many nights at the Winter Gardens, looking and listening to conversations, watching for who knows what, seeking a clue to his killer. Had I been that killer I wouldn't have returned after what I had done either but I had to try. He has never been found. Somewhere out there is a person who has that murder to account for when he passes on from this world. I pray he has repented and come to Christ before then, if he hasn't then I truly pity him. However much I thought of Jim I do not wish the fate that awaits him if he hasn't.

I have never forgotten Jim or the time we shared together.

So many memories of rides together throughout Devon and Somerset, where we discovered the wonder and freedom of riding without a destination, of going where the road leads and never caring whether we were lost or just taking another 'detour'.

Racing down the Cheddar Gorge flat out on our bikes or camping at Stonehenge watching the stars and dreaming of druid rituals under the full moon.

Building aircraft together then flying them. Talking about and meeting 'girls'. Always easier as a pair than alone, but in truth we were both happiest on our bikes out riding together to some unknown destination.

His life was just beginning, and then it was over, why? Because he dressed as he did, he was a young man living a fantasy and it cost him his life.

He was buried after the usual short service, his mother, sister and I attended. I have never been back to see his grave, it upsets me even now to remember his pointless death, but I think of him and remember the times we had together.

The early Greeks believed that as long as your name was remembered you were immortal so in a way Jim has never died, his name and his memory live on in me.

I had been bullied at school, beaten and starved to the point of hospitalisation by my mother at home, sexually abused at work, and left mentally scarred by what had been said and done to me over those years and by what I had seen. Now I had lost my only true friend,

Is it any surprise that I never trusted anyone again for such a very long time?

It would be more than 20 years before I found a friend like him again, before I would let anyone close enough to hurt me. Before I even began to trust again, for most of my life I believed I was better off not trusting, always keeping people at arm's length, never being truly open with anyone, especially women.

Moving on

After Jim died I had no reason to stay any longer with a family I had never felt close to or part of. I knew I had to leave and find a life of my own.

Partly out of desperation because of my past and poor reference from Curry's but also because of my love of aircraft I applied for training as an electrical fitter in the RAF.

At the interview I was asked about my sacking from Curry's and I told the truth. Yes I had stolen as I had admitted at the time but I had learned a great lesson and would never steal again. I told them about what my father had said to me and how ashamed I had been. After aptitude tests that showed I had a good understanding of basic electrical theory I was accepted for training.

Now for the first time I regretted my lack of schooling. To gain entry to the RAF I needed Basic English and maths to 'O' level standard, I had nothing.

Despite this because of my high scores in the aptitude tests, the RAF were prepared to take me pending the results of a six week intensive training course in English and maths. After a lot of hard work and very little time off 'You're here to work not enjoy yourself' I passed both and was accepted for training proper.

My love of physics had saved me, thank you Mr Gothry my old science teacher who opened my eyes to how great science could be and Mr Hammond Curry's engineer who taught me so much just from showing me how things worked. Without knowing it you had changed my life. Where would I have been, a thief with no future, with the past I had and no hope for a decent life, who knows.

An odd thing happened to me before I left finally for basic training with the RAF.

My mother and father came to see me off on the train. Dad shook my hand and gave me a short embrace. I think he was proud of me that day. My mother gripped my arm, lent in close to me and said 'Please don't be a tail gunner', she made me promise. It was a weird thing to say. To this day I wonder what was behind it. Had there been a man in my mother's past, before my father, during the war perhaps? Had she lost the man she really wanted? It would explain so much about her behaviour. I will never know but I still wonder about it sometimes.

After basic training, a time of left right up down and about turn, stand still, be quiet, run and walk became double and march. I learned to iron a shirt and make a bed 'the proper way' and to pack a locker 'just so'. After six weeks of this I was deemed sufficiently trained to progress to the next stage.

I was sent for technical training.

On the very first day I and my classmates met an old Flight Sergeant who was to be our principle trainer and tutor, he was no doubt highly skilled but teaching wasn't his forte.

I will always remember his introduction to the class.

We were sat like good little airmen all in rows and to attention, we rose smartly as he entered; he glared and waved us to sit again. For perhaps 30 seconds he looked at us, we numbered about 25 but at that moment I was sure he was looking only at me.

'You are here' he began 'to learn, it is my job to teach you, how am I going to do that? Well, let me tell you how my job works. I want you all to imagine you are a wall; there are 6ft high, 4ft high and 2ft high walls, some of you are rough walls, some smooth. I have a shovel and with it I throw shit at your wall, if you are a high rough wall it will stick, if however you are smooth no matter how high it will slide off and be lost, too short and it will just go right over, so what I want from you is to be a high rough wall where my shit hits and sticks, knowledge is like shit on your wall, you have to retain it for it to do any good'.

As a teacher now I cringe to think that was acceptable then but I must have been at least a 4ft rough wall because I learned and retained enough to qualify as a leading aircraftman (LAC) then later as a senior aircraftman (SAC).

I served throughout the UK rising in rank to junior technician (equivalent to corporal) and increased pay.

I saw Cyprus, learned to fly a glider, and discovered I had absolutely no talent for golf, went rallying and learned some judo and unarmed combat. In short during the first few years in the RAF I had a great time. I got married and did two tours in Northern Ireland. It was during the second tour that I arrived home on leave unannounced as I had been involved in a live fire incident that had resulted in a death. I can only say that a person was shot while I was on guard duty. I was cleared of any wrong doing and given home leave to get over the shock.

I arrived to discover my wife missing from home and a lot of the furniture seemed to have gone. It fell to a neighbour to tell me that the police had arrested her the previous evening for soliciting.

When I got her home from the police station we had a huge row. I didn't want to believe what I had been told but discovered that it had been going on for some time.

I have to admit to hitting her; she stood in front of me in our bedroom and admitted that she had used our bed right there to earn some extra cash. 'And why not' with me away she had been lonely and bored. I punched her once on the chin, hard; she went backwards over the bed bouncing on it and landed on the floor the other side. Had I been able to reach her I might have done far worse.

I left the house never to return and caught the first boat back to Northern Ireland. I got very drunk on that journey. I remember a lot of crying and then throwing up in my cabin at some point and to my shame leaving it when I finally disembarked at Belfast for someone else to clean up.

A divorce followed. To this day I have no idea what happened to the rest of the furniture that was still in the house, maybe she sold it, I really don't care.

One more interesting point, when I got back to camp I was arrested for the alleged assault of her while on leave.

She had telephoned the police and told them I had assaulted her and that I was a serving member of the armed forces. They contacted the RAF police (we called them snowdrops because of their white caps) who promptly arrested me. I was presented in front of my squadron commander the following day where after I had admitted the offence and explained the circumstances he found me guilty of behaviour likely to bring the good name of the RAF into disrepute and fined me I think £10. I thought this a small amount for the offence, more of a token fine than anything else. I think he sympathised with my position and fined me accordingly.

During the divorce the matter of an assault came up again as she seemed determined to pursue it. The judge looked at her having heard her explain why I had allegedly hit her, he asked if there had been any witnesses and there having been none told her that 'if' it had happened she had been very lucky. Many men would not have let it go at that, 'if' of course it had ever happened.

She was not happy. I was never asked about it, what would I have said? I would probably have lied and said it never happened, at that time like most people seem to I regarded the truth as something very flexible.

By now I had served some years in the RAF and was enjoying the variety of the work. I was, of course, used to moving about, something some of my colleagues found difficult having had, I suppose, more stable lives before they joined. I loved the work and the security that I gained. No problems with where to live eat or sleep. For a single male it has to be up there near the top as a way of life.

One funny story about my time in Northern Ireland and then I will move on.

I was again on guard duty, this time on the main gates when a telephone call came in alerting us that we were now on full alert and to close the gates.

The RAF Regiment who we partnered when on guard were immediately reinforced at all posts.

At this time I had no idea what was going on and was understandably nervous. Ammunition was checked and our alert status reported back.

About twenty minutes later an army bomb disposal land rover and a lorry turned up.

It seems that while doing a routine walk about one of the guards had seen a box with a wire attached to it fixed to the outside wall of the sergeant's mess. It hadn't been there the day before, so, assuming the worst as he should have he alerted security they raised our alert level and called the bomb disposal group.

The surrounding buildings were evacuated and some of the roads closed off.

After an examination of the box (I assume from a safe distance, I was still on the gate so didn't see any of this) they announced it safe.

It turned out to belong to the General Post Office, the forerunner of British Telecom. They had just the day before installed a new relay box on the wall.

Needless to say whoever had failed to record that fact heard about his error very swiftly! The next day with typical squaddie humour someone chalked on the box 'boom'.

At the end of my contracted employment period it had been my ambition to stay and make the RAF a career. By now I had also been awarded the General Service Medal 'Northern Ireland' a medal given for active campaign service, but I had also sadly lost mates to 'the troubles.' What it had to do with them I still haven't decided. Was it worth their lives to gain peace in the end? I hope so. Why were they there, did it really matter? They were there for the very sound reason the colour sergeant in 'Zulu' gives to a squaddie when he asks 'why us'? His reply, 'cos we're 'ere lad, and nobody else' it certainly wasn't their choice.

All in all I enjoyed Ireland, don't be put off by this account, it is a beautiful country with friendly warm people well worth a visit. I have been back since then and enjoyed every moment. The fishing in the South is fantastic.

With a shrinking service there were not sufficient places available for me to stay, so I returned to civilian life. For me this was another turning point in my life. The RAF had been good to me; it had taught me to be self-disciplined and had given me a trade and a pride in my workmanship that would stay with me all my life. 'If you are going to do a job, do it to the best of your ability' that motto served me well throughout my engineering career, gaining me the reputation of being both skilled and reliable.

Clubs and drugs

I settled in the South West of England and went to work for a plant hire company servicing equipment for hire. Day in day out the same lumps of concrete encrusted, dirty plant that needed cleaning and testing before it could be hired out again came to my bench.

After the variety of life in the RAF this was boredom personified. I had to find something better than this.

I was in contact with a friend who had left at the same time as me. He was also an electrical technician and had gone to work for a bus company in Wales, as an electrical fitter working on and repairing double decked buses.

I thought 'drop him a line and you never know there may be a better job in it' so I wrote to him asking how was life and any jobs going.

His reply was not encouraging; it seemed in the very first week he had nearly caused a walk out at the bus depot.

A bus had come in with a fault in the upstairs lights. Taff had found the problem and had started to remove the panel behind which the electrical distribution box he needed was located. A voice from behind him shouted "Just what the hell are you doing then? That's a fitter's job, not a spark's." It seemed Taff had discovered that wonderful British tradition 'demarcation'.

He had to wait the rest of the day until a mechanical fitter came along and removed the panel for him, all of six screws, 'And don't you be putting it back either'. Never mind I would look elsewhere, but nothing is ever as easy as it sounds, it would be quite a while before I found a job that suited me.

I had bought myself a bike, a Honda 400cc 'Dream' to get back and forth to work and for just enjoying at weekends. My love of bikes and the freedom I gained from riding helped keep me sane during the hours at work.

I had experimented with drugs in the late 60's before joining the RAF, but now I really went for it.

I had also joined my first bike club, a group whose sole purpose in life seemed to be to raise hell, drink and smoke anything we could lay our hands on and chase anything in a skirt.

I owned and ran several different bikes in this period. None were, as I recall, legal in one way or the other. It sure beat boredom.

I made friends and enjoyed the many rides out and parties. Girls knew what they were getting into going to parties with the club so sex was easy since most involved a weekend away there was never any doubt that they would end up sleeping with someone.

My lifestyle did nothing for my respect for women; I still saw them as useful but never to be fully trusted.

You can't trust a woman in the same way that you can trust one of your 'Bro's'- for many years I lived by this, trusting only those who had taken the same oath to a club as I had.

I had my first brush with the police around that time. On a night out with a few mates we came upon a diesel road roller 'I can start that' I drunkenly exclaimed and with no thought whatsoever I jumped up on it and after a short pause to turn on the fuel. I swung the starter handle and with a puff of black smoke away it went. For those of you who may be interested in such things it was a Coventry climax diesel, the one with the decompression lever on the top.

I looked down expecting to see my drunken mates but saw instead two police officers! Oh dear, I was arrested for the attempted theft of a motor vehicle and spent the night in the cells.

I was later fined but I can't remember how much by a bench of three magistrates who I am sure must have seen the funny side of the whole thing. I know I remember thinking at the time that I had got off lightly. This also taught me a lesson. My bro's in the

54

club would not have left me, they would have warned me, caused a distraction anything to prevent a fellow brother being 'nicked'. This served to reinforce my view that you could only trust your club bro's, nobody else.

In later years I have seen bikes run at speed at the police to distract them, windscreens smashed on police cars, even assaults on the police, all to protect a fellow Bro and aid the general escape of all. To not act would have meant expulsion from the club and 'disciplining' so that others would see what not supporting your Bros got you.

I have been lucky over the years I have never been caught for all the things I (may) have done. Close calls and a few desperate moments, but as I have said, lucky.

The only other time I was arrested and convicted of a criminal offence, it was really funny.

I was driving a Ford transit van and got pulled for speeding. That is until they read the tax disc and asked what model of Triumph motorcycle was it I was in. The end result was I got done for fraud. They took a dim view of me staining out details on the tax disc and adding other bits in!

As an individual biker I was vulnerable, it was very different when in a group.

The police have (or at least then had) an interesting attitude to bike clubs. Think about it, these were the days before personal radios when a PC was to all intents and purposes alone unless he was in a car that was radio equipped.

Would you, as a PC stop a lone bike and inquire for documents, or perhaps point out that they had been speeding? No problem really, now try stopping 10 or 15 bikes, all part of what was at the time regarded as a bunch of delinquents and trouble makers, that's another matter.

Most would be armed in one way or another and some weren't afraid to use them even on the police if they had no choice and no witnesses.

So, being human the police tended to leave bike clubs alone unless the behaviour became too outrageous. Then they would land 'mob handed' and have a field day issuing tickets and summonses like confetti!

Most of which got paid. Not so easy to ignore as they are now. If you didn't turn up in court a visit by the local police was guaranteed, not now. Now they haven't got the time or manpower to chase everyone who doesn't turn up, so the offence sits 'on the files' and pops up if you are stopped in the future.

I remember one occasion when I was riding with another club some years later we were on a 'run' to a party in the midlands somewhere. A full club turnout, as I recall about 30 bikes a lot two up with wives and girlfriends all laden with 'doss bags' (sleeping bags) and kit.

We had stopped in a village for a 'fag' break and probably a joint or two if that was your habit and to pick up drinks, grab a cuppa and stretch before moving on.

I don't know what started it but a couple of the guys got into a fight with some local lads. Nothing serious, a few punches got thrown, then those bro's in the vicinity piled in and the locals made a very hasty retreat.

As far as we were concerned nothing new, no harm done so let's just get out of here and forget it, nobody really hurt so no point in us making more of it. Honour intact we began to sort ourselves out to leave, then a 'panda' car arrived. I don't know what this PC thought he was going to do but he started by trying to get us all to turn off our bikes as he 'wanted a word'. This guy had watched too much TV! He stomped up and down getting nowhere and shouting. We all thought it was a complete laugh, and then two more cars arrived with older police in them. They and we both knew the score. They wouldn't take it like the young PC had so within minutes there was silence. The lads who had 'started' the fight were arrested and taken to the local police station that turned out to be about two miles away. What a great place we had chosen to stop! They were to be charged with assault and creating a public disturbance or some such.

Our president Animal was an old canny biker who although he had no liking for the police did respect them as an adversary and was well aware that in the final judgement they had the power of the state behind them.

At this time I held the rank of club secretary my job was planning runs general organisation etc. So he felt it was up to him and me to sort it out. I think he wanted to see if I would 'bottle out' because we were in direct conflict with the police, I didn't.

The whole club moved into the village and parked up, the lads had all been told to behave and not give the police an excuse for more arrests.

Animal and I went into the police station to see what was going to happen to our bro's.

It was one of those small country stations that you don't get any more. A few police covering the local area, perhaps one or two cars and several 'push bikes' or an old velo, (velocette motorcycle, very popular with the police and post office) maybe one or two cells for the local drunks.

The desk sergeant made it very clear that our bro's would be off to court in the morning and we would do well to be on our way, not a good outcome to a party weekend.

We sat outside for a while then Animal said 'ok if that's what they want we stay.' We then went back into the station to talk to the sergeant.

Animal was calm and polite this was a lesson he taught me when dealing with the police, it reduces the chance of getting 'nicked' and lets them think they are in control, it also stops them getting aggressive as they have no cause to. Anyway he outlined what would now happen, all the time saying how it wasn't what he or the police really wanted and he would like to just leave quietly as soon as he could but with two bro's inside he couldn't.

The club would stay in the area overnight so that they were around when our bro's were released after court the next day. A fine was all that they were expecting to receive and it was important that they knew the club hadn't just left them there.

This of course meant that they would have about 30 bikers including women in the local pubs getting 'pissed' that night and no matter how hard he tried there was no way that this wouldn't lead to trouble especially if the local lads who caused all this were found.

He admitted that the police could call in help to arrest the whole club if they had to but then what had started as a simple exchange of a few punches would escalate into something likely to make the papers, not counting the damage to local property and all the time and effort that would have to be put in by the police, paperwork, court appearances etc. and for what? Maybe these days it wouldn't happen with all our modern communication and zero tolerance but our bro's were released about half an hour later with a warning and told to leave and not come back.

We left, head up and with lots of attitude, all in all a satisfactory outcome for all. We were away and the police never saw us there again. Oh, and yes it was an excellent party made more so by the repeated, and of course, increasingly exaggerated telling of the story of our trip there.

One further point I would like to mention here. These days in a similar situation it would have escalated, I have no doubt of that. Today we take the zero tolerance route rather than what I feel is the more reasonable one. Reinforcements would have been called for, armed police and dogs, even a helicopter overhead. Riot shields and batons, in my day there was mutual respect. I have seen two bikers run across a road to intervene to protect a WPC from a drunk assaulting her. These days in the serious bike clubs it's them and us, with no respect asked for or given just another part of our society alienated and for what?

I sometimes think we have forgotten that a little 'give and take' goes a long way. Because some people live their lives differently from the majority doesn't make them criminals. Not just bikers but travellers, gypsies anyone who isn't part of the general herd is looked at with suspicion and that in turn leads to prejudice and injustice. It's that injustice that in my opinion can lead to the 'them and us' mentality and to criminal behaviour that in turn serves to reinforce the original mistrust and prejudice. Zero tolerance can mean just that...no tolerance for others who may be perceived as different to 'us'.

Drugs even in those days were easy to get and cheap, so I started a lifelong affiliation with cannabis, cocaine and amphetamine sulphate.

My violent upbringing had proved an advantage as I was no stranger to violence and almost embraced the release it gave me. The years passed and I rode with various clubs acquiring a reputation along the way of having a solid right hook and being handy with a knife, and not afraid to use it if the occasion demanded. I learnt to throw a knife well and could hit what I aimed at. I carry a scar from a knife fight as do several people who thought to try me, a dangerous time in my life.

What you see on TV isn't real. A knife fight is usually over very quickly. A thrust blocked then a slash or a lunge, someone cut perhaps once sometimes twice to make a point, blood and shock, and then it's over.

Nobody wants to kill, that's stupid. It's about image, being macho, not 'taking any shit', personal or club honour. Many reasons, but nobody with half a brain wants to do time for a disagreement that got out of hand.

Sometimes though it is necessary to go much further and really hurt someone. Maybe a drug debt or serious insult to the club or one of its members, then hospital can be the outcome for the victim. People have died in these situations. Nobody is ever allowed to get away with openly insulting the patch you wear that is the back patch or colours worn to show status of membership and club regalia. I know of at least one man who will never take off his shirt without seeing the scar that such an insult left him with, and perhaps thinking how lucky he actually was to have only that.

Also along the way I had acquired an addiction to amphetamine sulphate (or as it was better known Billy, Whiz or Speed).

At first I had been using it to get over the weekends and keep me functional for work on a Monday that quite rapidly changed into needing it just to be functional. I had been snorting lines and bombing (ingesting in wraps), however I now turned to the needle to give me the lift I needed.

This went on for a while until an ex addict helped me quit. A difficult time spent locked in his flat being weaned off the needle. He fought with me and I wrecked most of the place in wild moods of violence and depression, on at least one occasion coming close to being 'sectioned' under the mental health act when neighbours got involved, but he got me through it.

His name was Dick, known to all as 'Trash'. Some years later I heard he was using again and had committed suicide by laying his head on a rail line as a train passed. He was stoned at the time but I believe he knew what he was doing. He probably knew he was never going to kick his habit and just wanted it to be over. I remember well one occasion when we had a couple of ounces of 'squidgy' black an oily black cannabis so soft that he sat for hours making dope roses out of it, all sorts of sizes from little tight ones to full blown open floribunda, come the end we had quite a bunch and for some time it was 'dopes gone, I'll pick another rose!' I will always remember him.

To this day I have the track marks on my arms but have never touched speed again, partly for my own sake but also for 'Trash'.

I am like all addicts aware that I am still an addict, just not using. In the same way as an alcoholic can be on the wagon. To this day I feel the craving. I have been to parties and seen many people 'do lines', and yes the temptation is still there.

If you think giving up smoking is hard then you have no idea how hard it is to give up a drug that your body screams for every day for months on end. You wake begging for a hit and spend every waking moment trying not to want one and failing.

If you sleep then it is filled with nightmares. You sweat until the bed is soaked. The sudden and explosive need to open your bowls sometimes felt too late not giving you time to make it to a bucket or the toilet. Oh yes giving up is good for you in the long run but don't tell an addict that if he is trying to quit. He will probably ask 'how the f#ck would you know then?' And you had better have an answer or a smack in the mouth may well follow. It's a difficult time and a short temper is part of it so be warned. If you haven't been there don't judge.

I really believe that one of the worst things the government ever did was to change addiction from an illness to a crime so that doctors have to report it now. Many people have to go it alone if they don't want it on their record that they were once an addict and that discourages them from getting the help they need. Remember many countries won't let you in with a drugs record and it severely limits your job prospects. So addicts are alone with their pain other than the voluntary help that is available to some. Oh sure if you have money then off you go to rehab, but for the ordinary person it is a desperate time that many don't survive, for most it's back to the dealer, who being a nice fellow will usually give a free one because he knows quite well your back on the hook..

So many people don't understand. Druggies, not worth the air they breathe. Beneath contempt, gutter scum. Worthless, or are the majority just poor lost souls who need our love and our help.

Very few choose this route to hell, remember the saying and consider how fortunate you are not to have been on that road, 'There but for the grace of God go I'. Have you never made a mistake?

Finally because of the help I had been given and my own determination I was free of the addiction never to allow it to return.

As life went on I met and lived with a lot of different women, sometimes for weeks other times for years. They all had one thing in common though; they all had to put up with my mistrust and violence, and with my drug abuse.

From the beginning I adopted the attitude that if you don't trust or let anyone close then they can't hurt you. Why should I trust, every woman I had ever known had betrayed me in one way or another.

So my life became a sort of dotted line, a time with a woman then the inevitable violence sometimes just from me sometimes from both of us then a period alone until another woman came along to begin the cycle over again.

I was still living in the South West of England, had a reasonable job as a maintenance engineer in a factory and was living with a woman and two children. Life seemed good except for the violence.

She stood by me more than anyone ever had; she got me to tell my doctor the truth about what I was doing, to my surprise he wasn't even shocked he just told me that by admitting I had a problem I had taken the first step to coming to terms with it and stopping. He referred me to a psychiatrist who he said could help. I spent well over a year learning to accept what my mother had done to me as a child, trying to understand her and forgive her. The grounds of the psychiatric hospital were laid out with wandering paths, benches and flower beds. I spent many hours there just walking or sitting and thinking about what had been done to me and what I had done so far in my life. Eventually it was decided that I could now cope with my memories and with my guilt.

When I left therapy I was asked if I wanted to meet with my mother and try for reconciliation. I told them that I may now understand what my mother had done. Perhaps even the reasons for her behaviour. But no way could I forgive her. She had known what she was doing; she had made that choice not to get help but to continue. So no, reconciliation was the last thing I would consider. In fact she had better only hope that I never saw her walking down a road that I was driving on as I would run her over without a moment's hesitation. I really meant that, if I ever got the chance she was dead.

I don't think that was what they wanted to hear but it was the truth.

My hate for that woman would be with me for most of my adult life, festering deep within me, influencing me in ways I never imagined were possible.

No matter how hard I tried I could never stop my violence. The shrinks had helped me to understand but it had done nothing for my tendency to resort to violence to solve a problem.

One more point if you are one of those people who says 'violence never solved anything', then perhaps you should consider our own world history.

Where we as a nation would be without those who fought and died for all of us, to be as free as we now are?

Also read the bible, where did the state of Israel come from. Of me, people said 'you can never change a leopards spots' and they were correct, at this time I couldn't or perhaps wouldn't change.

Meningitis – what's that?

I was sitting watching TV one evening. It was during a 'good' period where the woman I was living with and I were getting along and life seemed okay. I developed a headache, over the next few hours it got steadily worse until my head felt as though it was going to explode. At some point I passed out and couldn't be woken.

I don't remember anything much only a vague remembrance of being lifted onto a stretcher, lights, all very confusing until I awoke two days later in hospital.

Meningitis, until then I don't think I had even heard of it much less worried about 'catching' it.

Well it seems I had been lucky; a treatment using an anti-biotic had been developed only 10 years before that's not so long in medical history terms until then the standard treatment was to drill a hole in the head to reduce the pressure and treat as a fever, not always very successfully.

I was well on the road to recovery and feeling good about life. One thing bothered me. I was visited by a guy from work. I had known him for at least six years but as he stood there saying hello I couldn't remember his name. I knew him but no matter how hard I tried his name eluded me.

After a few tests it became clear that although I had survived and recovered from the infection there was some brain damage.

To this day I can't remember people's names (proper nouns) easily so have various strategies to help me a 'Big guy called Robert became 'Bob the builder', Jan who does the petty cash became 'Jan Cash' with an association to Johnny Cash involved in there somehow, weird but for me it works.

I also have trouble with directions as I can't remember street names so again I have to use other methods to aid me. I navigate by buildings or prominent land marks. I also use a sat nav a device that for me has on more than one occasion been the difference between being lost and turning up on time for an appointment. Wonderful invention even if it was developed by the USA as part of a weapons system.

I have 'lumps' of memory missing, sometimes I will think back trying to remember an incident or when something happened but it has gone, it's a disquieting feeling to be missing parts of your life. I look at faces that I seem to recognise in the street but can't 'find' in my memory. Sometimes I have had people walk up to me and start chatting and I don't remember them, this has happened several times at bike rallies, people from before the damage was done, their names or what they meant to me gone forever.

I have learned to live with my problem and get on with my life being grateful that is all the meningitis did to me; it has done far worse too many others.

I still look back to this time and think how lucky I really was.

I came out of hospital and resumed my life, many people will never know about my disability; even some of my friends who know forget and wonder why I get lost occasionally. I have found myself driving down the wrong road on the way to work because I took the wrong exit at a roundabout without realising it. I have 'lost' my car several times having parked somewhere unfamiliar. I have been called stupid for doing this sort of thing. I once walked in on a conversation between my manager and a colleague that implied I was not to be trusted to do a particular job as I got lost too often. This attitude from a manager who worked for a company helping the disabled really hurt. However this is quite common for people who have a 'hidden' disability to suffer this kind of prejudice and is part of the reason I worked with the disabled and disadvantaged to try and help overcome this Victorian attitude to mental health.

I know what it feels like to be 'pre judged' by the so called 'able bodied', I have experienced the prejudice that has been common for the disabled but in the years since my illness there has been a huge improvement so that now it is an offence to discriminate against the disabled.

Sounds good but like all legislation until society believes in it then it will remain the law but often it is ignored and then it is very hard to prove one way or the other.

I hope by doing the work I now do that is teaching I am showing what can be achieved and that to have a mental disability isn't the end or a reason to give up and not work or to make a useful contribution to society.

I am a vocal advocate for the rights of disabled people, both physical and mental and spend a lot of my time trying to promote equal opportunities for all people regardless of their disability, race, sex or religious beliefs.

As part of my work I used to teach about equal opportunities to young people and try to show that prejudices are wrong and that we are all God's creations.

However there are some things that this society accepts and in fact now teaches as acceptable that I am unable to teach because the Bible, God clearly says it's a sin.

One such thing is active homosexuality.

However at this time in my life I didn't care one way or the other, I had no morals sexually, so do what makes you happy, we are only here once, enjoy it.

Goodbye to my father

My father died of cancer one November night, the greatest loss in my life, he had been ill for about a year and I had visited a few days earlier, he was in bed not really aware of his surroundings, he reached up and tugged my beard asking why was I wearing it, was I going to a fancy dress?

I think I knew then that his end was near. He looked so frail this big man I had known all my life reduced to skin and bone and looking so very tired, he was 52 but looked much older.

The local doctor was a good friend of my father, they both enjoyed coarse fishing and would spend time together just talking. I really don't know if they ever actually went fishing together but I don't suppose that matters.

He had cared for my father from the first awful diagnosis of cancer, the pointless surgery to investigate how far advanced it was and then the knowledge that he only had a few months to live typically he outdid them and lived a full year.

His death occurred in the early hours and he passed peacefully, he simply stopped breathing, although he had been in great pain for days before.

The doctor had been called a few hours previously and had given my father a large dose of morphine to ease the pain.

To this day I believe he helped my father more than he could ever admit.

I know that when I thanked him at the funeral 'For everything he had done' stressing the 'everything', he thanked me and said he liked my father and had done all he could to alleviate the pain and make the end peaceful for him.

I had the feeling that we both knew what the other meant but could not say it openly.

I thanked this man for his kindness and compassion. I won't get into the moral question of assisting someone to die, all I will say is when you watch someone you love in pain and know that all they will have until they die is more and more pain then it challenges how you look at 'assisting'. I truly pray it's a decision I never have to make.

For me he was all the family I had ever had or wanted, the only person I had ever loved or fully trusted.

I carried his coffin and said my goodbyes as I scattered his ashes in the river where he loved to fish. A little way upstream from a small stone bridge that was his favourite spot. Next to a reed bed, where bright blue dragon flies swooped over the water in the sunshine and birds sat in the overhanging branches of the willow trees. He was I felt now at last, at peace.

His loss affected me deeply; I closed off from people not allowing anyone to get close to me for a very long time. About this time my house subsided and I was made redundant from my job within a period of three months.

It was also about this time that I split from the woman I was living with, she had finally had enough and had realised that I wasn't going to change.

I now had nothing to stay for and I felt very little to live for. I had, as they say, 'had enough'.

Club Days, good bro's I could trust and cheap drugs.

Three shades of black Moto Guzzi, you could hear it coming
for miles! A beast, fast, reliable, and it handled well.

Early days, a 'Bitsa' bits of one and bits of another. It went well though.

'Baby' the knife I always carried.

'Dragons Breath' A 1966 Triumph Trophy 650cc, built by me in my dining room. At the Kent Custom Bike Show.

Honda 400 and sidecar, note the trailer and home built forks.

My first Moto Guzzi, a V1000cc Convert.

Chapter 3. Cat food, Starry Nights and my Saviour

On the road

Having decided enough was enough I packed those belongings I wanted to keep into a transit van, bought from a local scrap yard and repaired there on a work for spares basis.

Mostly tools, some books, my bike, photo's personal things, the rest I sold or gave away.

I said goodbye to my bro's in the club who sent me on my way with a massive lump of cannabis and headed north with my cat Doob sitting on the van dashboard watching the traffic.

I had converted the van by fitting a partition across it just behind the side door so that I effectively had an area where I could sleep, cook if it was wet and live.

A nifty paint job on the body completed the look, white with a 'day-glow' orange stripe around it, on the back doors was painted 'Service Van'. It also boasted an orange flashing light on the roof and a couple of rear facing spotlights.

As camouflage it worked very well, I was often looked at by the police on the road but all they saw was a guy driving a service van out working, it was as far from the standard traveller's van as I could make it.

In fact on at least one occasion when I pulled onto a travellers site I caused near panic, it was dark and this white transit van that looked like it could be police because of the orange stripe had arrived among them. Sorry guys, it was me.

We travelled together 'Doob' and I some fifteen months working where I could to earn diesel money, stealing it when I couldn't.

During this time my house was sold to a local builder at far below market value because of the subsidence and with the money my solicitor paid all my debts, the outstanding mortgage being the biggest worry.

He negotiated a settlement that meant that although I owed nothing it also meant I had nothing other than a huge weight of worry off my mind. I now had no money but also at last I owed nothing, it could have been worse!

Winter was hard, at times very hard, the next time you see some travellers in a van living the 'free' life you may want to remember that.

Not enough heat or food, the only water you have frozen and no fuel for the stove to melt it.

On one occasion I had to dig up a frozen turnip to eat when I couldn't catch anything. That I think was my lowest point.

Poor Doob lost weight and I think I was more concerned for her than I was for myself.

She took to sleeping in my doss bag (sleeping bag) with me; I often awoke to find her down at the end with my feet if it was a cold night.

I didn't mind, she was my friend and we only had each other.

I had a shot gun hidden in the van that came in very handy as a lot of rabbits found to their cost.

Farms lost the odd chicken and a good few eggs, potatoes etc.

I even considered sheep but couldn't bring myself to do it, not for any moral reason just how do you keep a dead sheep from going off in a van, even if you manage to butcher it.

Doob ate what I ate mostly and we both got thinner, but I did buy her decent cat food now and again as a treat when I had some cash from working or when I hadn't been able to catch anything.

To those reading this who know the score I will also mention lime in the streams for fish, baited hooks in the bushes for pheasants, about as far as you can get from environmentally friendly but effective, I did have money with me but it wasn't enough to live on so it was saved for occasions when times got really hard.

I shared a tin of cat food with her once when we were very hard up, whiskers isn't as bad as you might think fried up in a pan. I'm not sure she understood why she only got half the tin that time; I don't think she understood the concept of sharing!

Skips are really a fine source of food. The problem is you have to go into a town late at night to forage. It never failed to amaze me what shops threw out, damaged fruit, stale (that days) bread, milk, eggs, in fact as long as it hadn't been deliberately spoiled then if you were lucky you could eat well on this 'rubbish'. Now though most of these skips have locking lids, health and safety again? I don't really know. I do know however that if they are still throwing away as much as they used to, then it is a crime with so many struggling to make ends meet, and so many going hungry among our poorest citizens. An expired 'sell by' date does not make food inedible; in fact in most cases it makes no material difference. Surely we as a country could do something with all our 'expired date' food other than throw it in landfills? Why do we let people starve and still do this? What sort of society have we become? But I digress, I did warn you at the beginning I might but this is something I feel strongly about. What sort of society allows its old and its poor to suffer while the rich get richer and millions of tons of perfectly good food goes to land fill. It disgusts me, the sheer waste and heartlessness of it. One day we will all have to pay for the way we have treated our fellow man, what will we say then?

We got through winter, spring came as it always does and I found work on local farms, I seem to remember welding a lot of new tips on harrows and repairing various machines, my engineering skills kept me eating and gave me a value for the farmers I called on.

Farmers are a funny lot, they claim they never have any money but are always willing to barter, I worked for food, diesel, a place to park up for a few days and have a bath and wash clothes before heading off again.

As long as I had a few quid in my pocket then I was happy.

There is in North Yorkshire one lady who I am sure still remembers the three days I spent on her father's farm. She may not remember my name but we had a lot of fun together, smoking joints and making love under the stars before she sneaked back to her own bed in the early hours leaving me tired but very happy.

I don't remember her last name but I do remember her first name, Ruth, I was very tempted to try and stay there but the road called and I left to a fond farewell.

I have often wondered how she got on. Did she have a good life? I hope so. She wouldn't have if I had stayed, the violence would have eventually come between us and she would have regretted meeting me. At least this way we both have fond memories of those stolen two nights under the summer stars together.

A few months later I had moved across to the west coast heading I thought for the Lake District then up into Scotland.

To get there I planned to call in at Morecambe and meet a few of the northern bro's from the area.

The journey across to Morecambe was mostly just traveling another road. After a while you stop caring what it is called or where it leads, you're just traveling. I had spent a couple of nights at Killhope lead mines meeting with a few friends before I had to leave. Just drinking, talking and passing a joint around.

I had enjoyed the North East and wanted one day to return. The people are friendly and warm. The countryside is second to none for its beauty and wild places. I love the sea in all its moods. The wild waves that crash ashore driven by the winter gales busting upon the rocks in raw majestic spender. Or the warm summer winds blowing gently inland, laden with the smell of seaweed and ozone. Then there is the autumn 'fret,' the mist that drifts silently ashore to enshroud all about it in a blanket of silence and comforting isolation. It even rains less in the north east than almost anywhere else in the UK because of the Pennine mountain range. The rain coming ashore from the Atlantic is left in the North West. The lakes in 'the lake district' didn't get there because of a dry climate! The only other place I have been that can compare with the north east is the south west. Devon and Cornwall are beautiful counties but to my mind, now over populated. The roads are grid locked in summer. Water shortages and drought plague the residents and visitors alike. At times it feels as though you are living in one huge theme park.

So much of the reason to visit this truly beautiful area is lost because of the volume of visitors crowding into every nook and cranny, ironically searching for peace and isolation.

Now, before I upset some friends.

Yes, Scotland is also very beautiful, wild moors and mountains that rear up into the sky. Lakes (Lochs) as good as anywhere else, Glen Coe is staggeringly beautiful especially I think in winter with the snow-capped mountains. But, and I have to be honest here, you also have 'midges'. Horrid biting little fly's that can eat you over breakfast! They can drive you insane in clouds that surround your head and bite any bare flesh they can get at. I once asked a scot I met at a bike rally what to do about them, his reply to me, contemptuously "drink more"!

What did I really expect from a nation whose men run through waist high thistles in skirts (Kilts) with no underwear and play music with a sheep's stomach; the midges are probably frightened of them!

Settling down again

There was a small chapter of my club in Morecambe. As I have said I intended just to visit but after a few days of sofa surfing I was lent a caravan to live in. So inevitably, I settled down. I found a job, made friends and built up a steady income from dealing drugs as a side line to supplement my wages from working as an engineer in a local factory. However the main reason for dealing was that my own dope cost me nothing as it came out of the profits. You can't beat smoking for free.

The caravan was parked in a front garden. The lady who owned it was 'mam' to all the local bikers. She looked after us like a mother hen, any waif or stray was always welcome. She has passed on now but I bless her memory, she was a truly lovely caring woman who many Lancaster bikers owe a debt to. So that's where I was living, in mams caravan. One cold winter morning Doob got out while I was still asleep. Mam owned a Staffordshire terrier, Bernie, who, on this morning spotted Doob! He raced across the garden to catch her. Mam seeing what was happening snatched up Doob who promptly scratched her arms trying to escape. I had woken to the commotion and rushed out...I should have dressed first! The sight of a naked biker carrying a cat back to the caravan amused the neighbours no end, all 'Mam' said was 'I raised two sons; I've seen it all before!'

Doob in her own way decided where she wanted to be not long after.

I had been staying with some friends out in the countryside for a couple of weeks and Doob made friends with their little boy, they really got on well together she would roll over so he could tickle her, he found this hilarious and would laugh and laugh as he did it.

She had never been like that with anyone and when it came time to leave and return to the city we all knew she wanted to stay and the little lad was so full up at losing her I just had to leave her there. When I asked if he would look after her properly and always make sure she had her tea he answered so seriously that he would. I was sad but not as sad as the little one would have been and it gave Doob a good home where I knew she was going to be well looked after and she would be happy. I'm sure she knew as I gave her a final fuss when I left it was goodbye, and that her travelling days were over.

I eventually became Regional President of the North West Chapter of my bike club this is when I met Phil my second friend at a night club where he was working as a bouncer.

We were all going for a night out at a local nightclub when this guy on the door walked over. He actually had the nerve to threaten 15 hairy bikers! All wearing club colours, making it clear that if he had any trouble from any of us that night I would be the first one he jumped on. I liked him from that first moment and we became good friends.

He also had a quiet night!

The next day we were due to visit some of our bro's in Preston Jail so the last thing I needed was for any of the bro's to cause any serious trouble, we all had a good night, nobody got silly and I didn't get jumped on! Something I was grateful for as Phil was a big lad and fast with his fists as I was to see many times over the years I knew him.

As a club we had bro's on the 'inside.' While in the South West I had regularly visited our nearest then being Dartmoor. An awfully dreary and forbidding place, a sense of hopelessness about it that even for a prison is rare these days. Victorian built sitting in the middle of the moor in a shallow valley, almost hidden, but still menacing and as far as they could get from anywhere.

It scared the hell out of me just looking at it.

A high granite stone wall, bleak and forbidding, to say it had a haunted look about it is no exaggeration, if you have ever seen 'the hound of the Baskervilles' you have an idea of what I am talking about.

'The mire' of Dartmoor is a real place, it's a huge bog hidden under the tussock grass so that it looks firm until you step onto it then down you go, once in very little gets out alive, many sheep and a good few men have been lost to 'the mire' of Dartmoor. If you think of a shallow bowl then you have the landscape of Dartmoor and that is why 'the mire' exists, it can't drain.

I used to love hiking across it. Knowing the very real challenge it gave you. Sleeping rough with no tent just basic survival aids. Finding water and catching food. The moor can be your friend if you let it and learn some of its secrets. You will need a good staff to walk with though to help find the soft spots before you step on them, and to act as your 'ridge pole' when building a shelter. I still have mine, a trusty old friend that I cut in an ash wood in Wales and from which I will never be willingly parted.

Be careful, the weather can go from warm sunny to thick cold fog before you have time to look for landmarks. Then, all you can do is 'settle' and wait for the sun or a breeze to help you. Many people, usually holiday makers, have found to their cost how fickle the moor can be. They usually try to walk to safety, the biggest of all mistakes.

I spent two years as a volunteer with Dartmoor Rescue helping some very silly people off the moor when to be honest they had no idea how dangerous their situation had been. Go a few hundred yards away from the roads and you could so easily become disorientated and lost as many have found to their cost.

If they were lucky they spent a cold wet and miserable night on the moor or were found by Dartmoor Rescue, if they were unlucky they could die.

On the subject of HMP Dartmoor, I used to regularly smuggle dope (cannabis) into our bro's inside by having it stuck to my

79

hand inside a pair of fingerless gloves. The guards saw my fingers and never once asked me to take off the gloves. Isn't human nature odd, because they could see my fingers they assumed wrongly that I didn't have anything hidden in my gloves, worked every time!

I slipped off my gloves to shake hands with my bro when we met in full view of the screws (guards) and he took it off my palm into his hand, job done.

Phil and I rode many miles together in this country and Europe and both felt a bond difficult to explain, he could be a violent man prone to explosive bursts of temper as was I.

We respected each other because we both saw in the other the capacity for violence but also I think we both needed a non-judgemental friend.

He was good with his fists, I was good with a blade, neither of us took abuse from anyone and having someone you could trust at your back was a good feeling. I stayed for a while with Phil hiding in his attic for a period when the police would have liked to interview me for various reasons. Eventually I made the attic my home for some months. An interesting time spent hiding and 'keeping my head down' before moving on again.

I had met and was now living with another woman, again and again the cycle repeated over the years, meet live together, part.

A few years later the factory where I was working was going through a bad time and offered me voluntary redundancy. I had not long returned to work following an accident and time off. Entirely my fault and in those days health and safety was not as closely enforced as it is now so despite being off work because of it I got no compensation. I felt I had nothing to lose and the redundancy money would come in very useful. I had to try a new start again.

I was living with another woman who wanted to move away to try somewhere new to sort out our lives.

I had left the bike club after all the years as I felt it was part of the problem rather than the solution. So I took redundancy and moved to the north east of England remembering how much I had liked it while travelling. We stayed together less than a year before the inevitable distrust and violence drove us apart.

In the years following my move to the north east I found a job working as an electrician although it was a step down from my engineering qualification it paid the bills. It was a dirty cheaply run place, a factory producing chipboard. I had met and for some desperate reason married a female biker, maybe this was going to be different, she like me wanted so much just to be happy. It proved to be a complete disaster; she was full of violence and mistrust having come from a similar background to my own so our time together was short, violent and hurtful for both of us.

Looking back I really am surprised that neither of us ended up in prison having killed the other. She tried to stab me to death one night in my sleep. I awoke to find her holding a knife point to my throat; I just reacted and threw her off. On another occasion I choked her into unconsciousness. We both knew where this would lead so one day we parted, easily written but it was what most people would call 'messy', all the neighbours out watching as I threw her things into the street and she screamed abuse at me, then the police arrived and she collected all she wanted and left, I never saw her again. I can't say that the loss bothered me much at that time...there is an expression I had heard years earlier that described how I felt 'Dead dog syndrome' my dog has died, not to worry I will get over it by getting another dog. I am now ashamed by that but it was me then.

However in the years to come I was to think of her and regret the way I treated her and so many others.

It ended finally in a mutually agreed divorce. Since then I have heard she has married again to another biker and I truly pray she has found happiness, she wasn't a 'bad' person, just harmed by her life and in need of help and love. I hope and pray she found both.

I swore I would never marry again. Nobody would ever make me believe that marriage for me was a good idea. Why not just live together then when it all goes wrong at least you don't have to go through the divorce route. Just say goodbye and get it over with! Never again!

I stayed in the council house we had just moved into before we split up and tried to get my life on some sort of even keel. Some hope. Drugs and drink, and soon another woman filled my life.

I had by now developed asthma; I believe from the years in the dusty environments of firstly cloth and then paper and chipboard factories.

That and the other various injuries sustained over the years both from my lifestyle and work finally ended my engineering career. I have a back injury where I detached the muscle from my pelvis and both knees will never be the same again! Just out of interest I have also broken; one leg, one wrist, two fingers, one knuckle, both thumbs, my cheekbone, my nose three times two small bones in my foot, my ankle, a rib and have been concussed twice, had my teeth knocked out and pulled and torn various ligaments, not a bad score all things considered!

What to do? I had bills to pay, a life I wanted to lead and suddenly I was out of work and for the first time in my life I was an 'unskilled' worker.

This is a tremendous shock for someone who has always been able to fall back on their skills and experience to put food on the table, and fuel in the tank. Now there was emptiness, a feeling of uselessness, what was I going to do? I had nothing; no skills no trade what could I do.

For a few months I sat back, it was summer and I had money in the bank and the 'dole'. I was as always dealing to help with the income but I was bored.

I got more and more used to doing nothing and staying stoned. 'Start the day the wobbly way' became my motto as I lit the first joint of the day for breakfast.

This went on for a while. At the same time I was running out of money, one day it had gone and all I had was the 'dole' and the dope, the problem was this was also getting less profitable for the same risk. I considered coke or fet (cocaine and amphetamine sulphate) but because there were several dealers in the area I didn't want to step on anyone's toes, remember, I had to live there.

I did some 'cash in hand' wiring jobs for people, went grouse beating, even helped build a garage for someone, in fact anything I could find to raise a bit of cash.

The weeks went by and soon I was without a car and couldn't afford to tax or insure my bike so that went as well.

One day I woke up to the realisation that my life was going nowhere and if I didn't do something about it this was all I would ever be, a drug dealer on the dole. I have been a lot of things in my life but I have never been idle. I had to work but how and at what?

Something had to change so with the help of a charity who assist disabled people find work I was sent to a college for the disabled to train in a new trade.

I was going to be a commercial horticulturist. No more factories for me, out in the good clean air, no more noise or dust every day, bliss. Oh those Rose coloured specs!

Back to school

To those who say 'I'm too old' believe me you're not!

Two admissions; Latin is horrendous to learn and I hated working outdoors in the wet or the cold. Too many memories of servicing tower cranes in the winter, what a job that was, lovely in the summer looking out over the city or countryside, but winter was another story, freezing wind, snow and ice and everything you touch is frozen solid sheet ice. Put down a spanner and it freezes to the steel deck if it isn't bone dry. <u>Never</u> unclip that safety line in winter, in summer you stroll around up there but only a complete fool would in winter. The ladders are steel, your boots slip and slide, anyone who says that it doesn't scare them in winter has never slipped climbing one of those ladders and grabbed hold with a grip they didn't know they had, yet. You feel so alone when you sit out on the end of the jib, you can hear the frame cracking and creaking in the wind, sometimes the sway is measured in feet, then it really moans and groans!

Don't get many of the bosses bothering you there!

But to be honest it's a young man's job, lots of ladders and they play hell with your knees, and after a few years go by it gets tiring hauling tools and spares up and down.

The last time for me was in Exeter working on a new multi storey car park.

It was January, wet, cold and a wind that down south they call 'lazy' because it goes straight through you, it's too lazy to go around.

It was a big site, lots of opportunities for a little extra bonus.

As a site maintenance engineer I was there a lot of the time alone, after a while the word spreads that if you call in on a Sunday and talk to the chap doing the servicing you can get just about anything very cheaply.

The biggest item ever to go missing was a dump truck; the guy paid and just drove it off site. Where he went I have no idea, it looked so obviously stolen but nobody saw a thing they said when the police asked.

Mostly it was pallets of bricks or bags of plaster, stuff that nobody really counted too carefully.

The cold finally got to me and I said enough and moved on to a warmer, but less well paid job.

This habit of moving and learning new jobs was to serve me well in the future as I found when I went to college.

A lifetime of learning new machines and their associated manuals now proved to be an advantage, most people lose the habit of learning as they grow older, but I hadn't.

I couldn't do anything about the Latin but by training as a commercial horticulturist rather than landscape or nursery I would spend my time developing new breeds, growing thousands of plants for the commercial outlets, big DIY shops etc. Rather than digging in the wet mud to plant cabbages or prune trees, sorry to all you horticulturists – aka 'garden designers' out there but it isn't for me.   My environment is warm, dry and humidity controlled. What plants like is pretty close to what suits us so it seemed like a good idea to me.

I love watching plants grow, I know that sounds silly but have you ever really looked at a plant and really watched it grow? Have you ever wondered at the complexity of life and how it all got here? Or tried to understand why it grows as it does, how does the environment effect it, what food does it need, how much light or CO_2, how much heat and moisture? Or marvelled that a seed so tiny that it blows away in the wind can grow into a 90 feet high tree, or lie dormant for years waiting for the right conditions to burst into life?

A shoot shows its head for the first time, you know all is well and before long hundreds or thousands of its cousins will do the same, life has begun down there in the warm soil.

Straining to reach the light the seedling grows taller, the first seed leaves develop; photosynthesis begins and the stem hardens to support the now rapidly growing plant. Below the soil, out of sight roots probe for water and food, providing an anchor for the plant above. Eventually flowers burst into glory displaying themselves for propagating insects.

Left to their own devices most plants will grow tall to reach the sun and have a limited number of flowers, not what the market wants.

Look at the roundabouts on your drive home, who grew those plants that are all in flower at the same time? Most are the same size making for easy planting in beds where they can be displayed to their best. Hundreds of thousands of plants each year planted in private gardens, who grows them all? We do the commercial horticulturists of this world.

I worked hard to learn my new trade, I can't help it, remember, and 'do it to the best of your ability' still dominates the way I work. Latin however still eludes me!

I was working toward a level 3 qualification the highest 'working' grade, after this the qualification tends to become more 'managerial' in nature.

I wanted to grow plants but I also wanted to be given some responsibility and have 'a foot on the promotion ladder'. Only by being good at what you do can you hope to progress and I wasn't made to 'just coast along'. In my final year having taken and passed my level 2 qualification I was assisting in the training of the level 1 students, teaching them what I had learned only the year before.

I had to work even harder to stay ahead and there were always the questions I couldn't answer.

In theory I could ask my tutor, but his answer was always 'Go and find out'. Only after I had done this would he confirm my answer so I quickly learned not to bother asking but to find out in the first instance and then check my answer with him. I now appreciate what a good tutor he was, he not only taught me horticulture but also to search the text books effectively.

I qualified at level 3 and went to work in a nursery run by a national charity that help the disabled and disadvantaged.

Well you would think I was happy wouldn't you? Not so. Because I was also teaching people horticulture I was aware that I was not a good teacher and if I was going to be then there was only one way to go. I was heading back to school again. In this instance Sunderland University to learn how to teach properly.

That was fun, the oldest student in the class!

However I am once again getting ahead of myself so we will leave it there for a while, we will however return to Sunderland University and teaching later.

A house, and a bike

Phil and I had both mellowed somewhat as the years passed and we had kept in touch each visiting the other at irregular intervals. He had several relationships and went through the break-ups and pain that caused. My life was similar in many ways but through it all we remained good friends and gave each other what help we could.

He was still living in Morecambe and I was on the East coast but we visited each other and kept in touch. I was still using dope (cannabis) on a regular basis and dealing to pay for my habit.

In 2002 my mother died.

For me, I am now sorry to say, this was not an occasion of regret. The shrinks had helped me understand back in therapy that her behaviour was probably due to the loss of my brother but I could not forgive.

All I could think was "she's gone at last". Maybe that was wrong but it was how I felt and I won't lie in this account. I was I think relieved, that I would never have to see her again. She would never be able to hurt me again, never beat me, and never make my life seem worthless again. Part of me recognises that she was my mother and I should have felt some loss at least, however I didn't until years later when I could finally forgive her.

I could not be found by my family in time to attend the funeral they said. I was only contacted through a search agency when it transpired that my sister and her family could not sell my parents' house. My father had left half of it to me in trust when he passed away, thus ensuring that I would not be cut out of any settlements.

I was amazed that even after all the time that had passed since his death he had reached out to help me.

With the money left to me I bought my house, paid all my debts and bought the first brand new motorcycle I had ever owned.

For a while I was content with my life, I had a good job, a steady girlfriend I was living with, and no debts. I holidayed in Spain, rode my bike through Europe, had good friends but somehow I was never truly happy. I felt incomplete, but I had no idea why, no idea what was missing from my life.

I was still violent but by now had learned to control it to the extent that as long as I wasn't shouted at or confronted head on by a finger pointing woman I could walk away. But if pushed I would explode into violence as bad as at any time in my life before.

By now I had given up any hope of true happiness, I would look at other couples and wonder why they were so in love and happy after being together for many years. I suppose I knew the answer but wouldn't face up to the fact that as long as I was violent I would never know that happiness.

Somehow I was always alone inside even when I was 'with' a woman in a relationship however long. I could never let them close to the real me buried deep inside. How many times in my life had I begged for the violence to leave me alone?

Twice I had attempted suicide not as a cry for help, for real, twice I had failed through no fault of my own.

The first time I took Paracetamol and sleeping tablets, some I threw up before passing out, nobody was due to call but some friends did and seeing me lying across the bed (ground floor flat) broke the door down and got an ambulance. That was the day I joined the 'funnel club'. It's an odd sight to see your stomach going up and down by itself as the nurses fill it from a funnel and then drain it out again into a bucket to flush out the drugs.

The other time I got drunk and went to a local (high) bridge intending to sit in the quiet and think. I looked, I thought, then I climbed over the edge onto a narrow ledge closed my eyes and was grabbed by a guy walking his dog. He wouldn't let go and finally the police arrived and I got lifted back. By then I had no fight in me I just gave in to the inevitable.

I was taken to hospital and interviewed by a young man in a white coat, with a pleasant attitude who only wanted to help me. I had met his type before in therapy, so I told him all the things he wanted to hear. It had been a stupid drunken act and no, I didn't mean to kill myself and I was so grateful to every one for helping me and I really was a nice guy who had just lost it for a moment because of the pressure of life.

They kept me in overnight and after another similar interview in the morning let me go.

I remember he wore a small gold cross on his left lapel. I thought its ok for you mate you have no idea what the real world is like.

You see I thought because he wore the cross he was just another bible basher who lived in some sort of dream world where there was a god who would help you, love you, look after you, what a mug, I knew better, there was no God.

My whole life I had denied the existence of God and would even challenge him to prove his existence, show me and I will believe in you. I would actually argue the point that he didn't exist, having seen first-hand the pain and suffering caused in Ireland when two religions don't agree, the needless killing on all sides. I shunned all mainstream religions.

As I had become a better engineer my interest in science had grown, how the universe had formed, why are we here, what happens if we reach light speed, how does an atom form? Questions that led to more questions, nowhere in all the reading I did was there a need for a god to make things work.

I had tried Tarot cards, crystals, paganism, even magic. I know now that even then I was searching for spiritual peace. I had even written a poem dedicated to riding behind the devil when I died, it had been published in a bike magazine but nowhere in my life was there space or reason for a god.

One evening sitting with Phil talking bikes he showed me a picture of an Indian motorcycle he was going to buy. He had just sold his business and was planning to collect the bike from the factory in America and combine the visit with a holiday.

There was no way I was going to let Phil go to America without me, I still had money from my Father so could afford to go.

We finally settled on flying to the West Coast and spending six weeks riding across the country before shipping the bikes home from the East Coast. Phil was to keep his bike I was to sell mine to help finance my costs.

This I thought would be the best riding experience of my life. We did make one mistake though. We both quite naturally agreed to take our current girlfriends with us, as it turned out we would have had a far better time if we hadn't, some people are made for riding thousands of miles, others aren't.

I did not foresee that it would also lead to me returning a completely different person, and be the beginning of a new life for me.

America

In September 2003 we arrived with girlfriends in San Jose, California, at this time for me God was at best an urban myth.

America, what can I say? My first impression was of huge cars and a culture that superficially looked the same but was very different to the one I had left in England. The six lane highways, the rush to be somewhere that seemed to be the norm and oddly, very few people walking, and of course the best coffee in the world.

We collected our bikes from the dealers two days later having got over the jet lag and then very carefully on the wrong side of the road went to a huge store (Blackbird Outdoors). 'If we don't sell it you can't buy it' I know what they mean but it has always amused me. There we got all we would need to camp and survive on our journey across America.

Our plan was simple, head north through California on the coast highway then east through Oregon heading for the east coast and Washington. We deliberately under planned the route to be able to go where the road led us. We wanted to really experience the ride not just have a touring holiday, we knew there were risks in this but by doing as we did we never knew what the next day would bring us. Looking back I don't regret that decision as I saw parts of America and met people that I never would have, had we been running to an itinerary. Our only constraint was we had to be at the airport in six weeks.

Leaving San Francisco my bike a 1300cc Gilroy Indian decided to dump the engine oil over the back wheel. A telephone call to the dealer soon identified the cause as an over filled oil tank. Since the 'extra' had already drained itself we cleaned up the wheel and brake disc then headed out of the city, our journey had begun.

That first night was really good. We found a good camping ground and headed into a small local bar. After a few beers I wandered off to chat to a guy at the bar. Long hair, tinted shades and western boots! We did the usual, where you from, how long you here for? Then we wandered outside for a smoke. When I returned we had another beer or two and left. Phil was so impressed when later I pulled out half an ounce of dope and proceeded to skin up that is put a joint together. 'Only you' he said 'could travel across the Atlantic and score in the first bar we went into'. What could I say? Some have it, some don't.

By the end of that first week we had settled into the bikes and a routine. Ride until we wanted to stop or saw something we wanted to see, set up camp and eat, relax and talk about the day. This was a good time for all of us. Watching the sun go down, listening to strange bird calls or animals we couldn't identify in the night, looking up to see the stars in unfamiliar places fantastically bright with no light pollution to dim them. I have never seen the Milky Way so bright and clear. It was odd though to see all the stars I was familiar with displaced in the sky.

Later that week we stayed at a motel in Tahoe to do the washing and have a night of air conditioned luxury. This was to become a pattern, ride for maybe a week then stop and treat ourselves. Early the next morning I went fishing in the deepest lake in North America, a dormant volcano. One lake trout later back to the motel and load up the bike. I swapped the trout at a local restaurant for breakfast. Later that day we set off again, climbing switch back roads up the mountain. Bend after climbing bend with an ever increasing unguarded drop off the road edge. Very scary but what a view from the top, miles of forest and clouds as far as we could see with Lake Tahoe, where I had fished that morning, far below glistening in the afternoon sun. We paused for a while at the summit letting the bikes cool. They had been working hard on the climb fully loaded and two up and needed a rest. A drink and a cigarette later we set off again. This time, for the descent down the other side of the mountain into the deep redwood forests of Oregon, I didn't know it but my life was about to change forever.

The descent began easily enough, fifty or sixty yards then bend, another fifty or sixty yards and another bend, hairpin bends hugging the mountain first right then left, steady but steep. I had held the bike in third gear (mistake) rather than second to let it run cooler. The result was I didn't have much in the way of engine braking; normally not a problem, all I had to do was change down, but with the Indian to do so meant going through neutral and risking not being able to find a gear. Four or five bends later I knew I was in trouble.

I had lost the rear brake due to oil mist from the engine a repeat of the problem I had in San Francisco this time due to running so hot on the climb. The front brake was now all the way back against the handlebar grip and the fluid had boiled as I attempted to at least slow the bike's progress. I now had no brakes. I decided not to try to change gear, had I missed the change I would have had no control whatsoever and, however slight, I wanted to at least feel as though I still had some.

Phil must have been very surprised when I passed him on the next straight and threw the bike into the next bend just about on the limit of lean, side stand scraping on the road. Ahead of me, speed still climbing, was the bend I knew I wouldn't make.

Now I had two choices, dump the bike by that I mean lay it down deliberately and kick free as it slides on the road or hang on and go over the edge of a huge drop. I shouted to my girlfriend on the back "we are coming off, I'm dumping it, bail when it hits." I knew it was going to hurt, maybe badly, but better broken bones than the death that certainly awaited us if we went over the edge.

I heaved the bike over as we entered that bend down as far as it would go, metal grinding on the road as it began to slide. I could feel the back end start to move out as the tyre lost its hold my brain was screaming NOW bail now. I couldn't.

Ahead of me the edge and I couldn't believe what I was seeing, a patch of ground, maybe ten yards long, gravel covered, incredible, but too late. The bike was now completely out of my control the back end breaking away. I had no illusions about how long I had left before the inevitable happened.

To this day I can only recount what happened next with complete awe.

I remembered a face, a guy we had met in Tahoe it was just a flash of him nothing more. He was a local doctor and his parting words to us had been 'God go with you'. I don't remember my reply, probably thank you or something similar. At this point I couldn't move my hands it was as if they were being held. I really wanted to let go, I was trying to bail and I am not prone to panic. The bike swung on the road, came up, slowed and ran impossibly straight into the waste ground and stopped upright and without any slide or attempt to dig into the loose gravel, or any input from me. This happened in micro seconds but I can still see and feel every part as if in slow motion. I couldn't believe what had happened.

Phil arrived, his first words 'How the f#ck did you stop it?' I could only reply 'I didn't'. He looked at me as though I was stupid.

There it was stopped after all; I got off and for the first time in my life said 'thank you' to God and meant it. I just sat for a while after that thinking and frankly getting over the adrenalin rush until I could ride again.

It had taken God many years to answer my irreverent 'show me and I will believe'. Now he had, in a way I just couldn't ignore. I knew what had just happened <u>couldn't</u> happen but had. I have ridden bikes all my life, I know what they can and can't do. I'm not, as I have said, prone to panic and this was not my first 'off' by any means. I have ridden cross country, raced bikes and ridden big touring bikes all over the UK and Europe. What happened was not possible from where the bike was and at the speed we were going or the direction of the slide, never mind the fact that it was well overloaded with bags, two up and without any brakes.

Phil saw it happen and just couldn't believe what he saw. He would never talk about it other than to say, if pushed, 'it was really weird it just stood up'. As a self-confessed atheist and a lifelong biker he would have loved to be able to explain it but never could.

On that mountain there is one, and only one, area that isn't a sheer drop. That was it, a bit of an overhang not even big enough to park two cars.

I went up that mountain convinced God did not exist. When I came down I knew He did. No doubts no ifs buts or maybe's I knew it as a fact. We refilled the front brake master cylinder and came off the mountain. To this day I still don't remember that part of the ride. We finally came to a small town, Bend; where there was an Indian dealer who we hoped could repair the damage and sort the oil leak problem.

They looked at the bike at the dealers and yes they could sort it but parts were a problem, it would take a few days. I remember asking if there was a motel or anywhere to stay locally when a voice from behind me said 'why don't you stay with me'. That was when I met Dave, a big and bearded American biker. He had heard my tale of woe and decided to help if he could. Just like that he decided to help me, a total stranger. We left the bike with the dealer and Dave took us back to his place to meet his wife (she won't mind I'm always bringing people home) Annie. He was right, she didn't mind, in fact we were made very welcome as if we were old friends. A lovely couple living in a trailer park, he was an ex drug addict she an ex alcoholic and both born again Christians. This was Friday. I sat outside that night and for reasons I couldn't then explain told Dave my story. My childhood, the years of drug abuse and violence and what had happened to me at Tahoe on that descent. I remember him smiling at me then, he didn't say a lot but quietly told me he would be in church that Sunday 'would I like to come?' I said yes.

That Sunday in a small evangelist church I stood and told the people gathered there my story and asked Jesus to come into my life. The pastor Jay put his hands on me and asked if I truly accepted Jesus as my saviour, if I was willing to give my life to him. As I answered yes, I knew I had been saved. Nothing can describe the joy I felt and the strength that flowed into me. As tears that I couldn't stop ran down my face I stood there changed forever.

Before we left a few days later Dave asked a favour of me. He was a Vietnam veteran. He took me to meet a friend he had served with who was dying of cancer. He knew he only had weeks left.

Mike said he had a 'real big favour' to ask. It was a moment before he spoke again. I could see him making up his mind to ask and I was a bit concerned what this 'favour' was going to be. Finally he said 'I lost a lot of bro's in Nam, good men who never came home. I'm dying now so it won't be so long before I join them'. He paused and looked at me. 'Will you be going to Arlington Cemetery before you go home?' I told him I was. 'When you do, would you go to the Vietnam memorial wall for me and tell them I'm coming?' what could I say, of course I would. He told me some names to look for and made sure I wrote them down. I took his hand and gave him my word before God it would be done. It was a very emotional moment for all of us. Before I left we prayed together.

Phil and I left Bend the next day on our journey across the USA.

We rode across deserts that went on forever and over mountains that seemed to touch the sky. Temperatures that ranged from highs of 38degC down to 0degC in the course one day, from sea level to thousands of feet up and everywhere there was God. How could I have ever denied him it was so easy to see him now and all his work. I prayed every day and thanked Jesus for saving me. More than once I asked 'why me'. I was so grateful but I'm nothing special so why had he bothered? The truth, that I didn't see then, is that to Him we are all special. Sinner or saint, he loves us all and wants us to come to Him and his love.

I met a mechanic in Idaho who saw the simple cross I was wearing on my leather waistcoat. I didn't know his name we were just passing in a workshop while my bike was being serviced. He said 'God Bless' as he passed, so naturally as if he was saying 'good day'. As we were leaving later he walked up to me and shook my hand and wished us well for our journey. It was then I saw his belt buckle 'Jesus Rides with me'. I never got his name but I will always remember him.

I didn't know it then but I had begun walking the path that seven years later would lead to my baptism in the river Wear in County Durham and the beginning of another phase of my journey as a Christian.

I still carry a picture of Dave and Annie with my Bible and have the copy of the New Testament he gave me as a parting gift that I read as I travelled across America.

Yes, I went to Arlington and I kept my word. I told his bro's he was coming and said the words he had asked me to. I couldn't help it afterwards I sat and cried alone on a bench, nobody bothered me as I prayed for them all.

I must mention Medford, Washington State. We were invited to a party with a bike club called the 'Medford Riders' at the local fire station. It wasn't until we had been there a few hours that we realised these guys had been on duty on 9/11/2001.

They were so matter of fact about it. It was later when they got to know us that they opened up about that day. They lost members of their crew there; a memorial garden commemorates the firemen lost. The stories they told chilled me. The things they had seen, and had to do, most had to have counselling afterwards. Brave men. They asked us if 9/11 had put us off coming. We explained that we believed very strongly that if terrorism is to succeed it has to stop the ordinary person. If we stop travelling and live in fear then they have won. In a way it was our way of fighting them, no we were never going to be stopped doing anything by fear. Terrorism should never be a legitimate means of gaining political power. However as we all know today's terrorist is tomorrow's freedom fighter. How many world governments now in power came about by what was at the time called terrorism? Who are we to judge, isn't all killing wrong?

One other bike club I have to mention. How could I not? This, even after my life as a biker and knowing the code most bikers live by, surprised me.

Phil and I were on the freeway heading for Washington when all his electrics failed and he rolled to a halt. Luckily we were near an exit ramp, so we gave it a push and rolled down to a bar just off the freeway. It was just getting dark.

A few moments later a bunch of bikes arrived, all big and mean looking bikers, every one of them black every one of them looking at us.

I have to be honest, I thought 'this is trouble' as it turned out I couldn't have been more wrong.

So, firstly, an apology to all of them. I did what I hate to see others do. I pre judged another person based on their colour. I am truly sorry and ashamed for doing that and ask your forgiveness.

They introduced themselves 'The lonely ones', 'you guys broke down?' We explained who we were and what we were doing in America. We explained that we had ridden 4,500 miles across their country, and were off home to the UK in a few days' time. To cut a long story short, they put us in a motel and partied with us into the night. The next day, they loaded the bikes onto a pickup, and then took us to the nearest Indian dealership. Don't misunderstand me here, this wasn't a few miles down the road, it took us all morning to drive there!

Some were Christian, some weren't. They were all bikers who like us respected other bikers and clubs, old school.

In payment for all they did they wouldn't even take gas money finally they accepted an Indian Centenary badge available only to Indian owners for their trophy wall and a card from Phil and me giving our club details. Nice one guys, ride free, God bless you all.

Tornado alley

What a name and what a description.

We were camped on a small hill in Idaho under some trees for shade when the wind began to rise. During the day as we were riding we had seen small twisters in the distance and watched

99

them run across the countryside impressed but not feeling threatened in any material way.

We had decided that they were not dangerous, as long as we kept out of their path. Good plan! I know it seems stupid now but at the time it never occurred to us to check the local forecast or ask advice as to where a good camping spot was in this weather. Stupid tourists how often in the past had I said that of visitors to Dartmoor and here I was just as stupid.

Anyway as I have said the wind began to rise. It got darker and began to rain so we headed for the tents and zipped up tight and settled down for the night and tried to sleep. After all this was not the first rainy night we had experienced.

There in the far distance, was that a train I could hear coming? Far off the roar of engines or was it a big truck working hard to pull its load?

As I listened it got closer, then it arrived, a wind that howled and in a second pushed the tent flat and dumped hundreds of gallons of rain. In moments there were inches of water in the tent, flashes of lightning and huge bangs filled our world. We pushed the bags and all our kit to the front the into wind end of the tent and were lying on it all to keep the leading edge of the tent down to stop the wind from getting under it and lifting it. Had that happened the results don't bear thinking about. We would have been tossed like toys and smashed just as easily. During the whole time about five minutes in all, I was afraid of what was happening and did what I had to do to survive, at one point I had to physically restrain my girlfriend who was close to panic.

Throughout, I had faith in Jesus and believed that even if I was going to die I was going to be all right. It was very odd to feel like that. All my life I had been alone, with nobody to rely on or trust. Now all that was changed, I knew He was there with me; I would never be alone again.

It passed, the rain stopped, we crawled out to a scene I will never forget. The corn in the fields around us that had looked so tall and impressive when we arrived was torn to shreds and flattened, thrown in piles against the tree trunks on the edge of our small hill, filling the ditch by the road. It looked like a giant had thrown it all about in a rage. The 'not so jolly green giant'!

Water everywhere, running away to drains and gullies that we couldn't see. Worst of all a tree not 20 yards from us split by lightning, burst down its trunk and ripped open, still steaming. Both bikes incredibly still standing, if now a good bit wetter and very dirty from blown mud and leaves. We had survived. We were not only alive but from what we could see more or less intact. Everything we owned was soaked, all our paperwork was sodden and the bikes were a mess. We had been so fortunate, I thanked God. Phil said we had been lucky and moaned that he had lost so much and that all his kit was soaked. There seemed no point in saying at least you are alive! That day was spent sorting and trying to save all we could. That evening we booked into a motel and spread it all on the bed to dry.

We phoned Dave and Annie that night because we thought they might be worried. We had been watching CNN news on TV when they ran a report from where we were showing 'the extensive damage, worst so far this year'. Yes they had also seen it, and were quite impressed when we told him where we were!

Six days later we were in Washington preparing to come home. 4,700 miles and six weeks had been great for us but Phil and I were both tired of listening to the moaning and complaining by the women we were with. They wanted to go home. I can't say I blame them really. Six weeks is a long time to sit on a bike and neither of them had 'a wander lust' like Phil and I.

We would have been happy to turn around and spend the next six weeks riding. Maybe south along the east coast or north to

Canada, who knows? But no, we came home. I wish we hadn't. We should have said okay you go home; we will be back in six weeks.

I remember on the flight home it felt as though we were leaving 'early' and Phil and I talked 'Well, where to next time Bro?' there is no doubt in my mind that there would have been other long distance rides, we had both loved the riding, the open road without a schedule or a destination, but next time just us, no girlfriends, we were both adamant about that!

This was to be one of the last times I rode with Phil; his life was coming to its end, although, of course, neither of us knew it at the time.

After America

After we got back I suppose, understandably, we needed a break from each other. It had been tough at times in the USA and we had almost fallen out more than once so a bit of a break seemed a good idea. I went home as did he, and for a few weeks we ignored each other.

We did a rally together to show the bikes and try to find a buyer for mine. Phil had paid half towards it on the promise of when it sells he got his money back. Finally it did sell but only after a lot of heart ache and effort and at a lot less money than either of us had anticipated. In fact I had been offered more for it while I was still in the States by a dealer on the east coast, and that didn't take into account the shipping costs, import tax or the work we had to do to get it to pass the Single Vehicle Approval test. A test applied to all imported vehicles to ensure they comply with UK legislation. Not my best ever investment but such is life! When it sold Phil took what he was owed and gave me the balance.

I was still living in the north east, life went on as before. I went to University to train as a teacher. It took me two years to gain my teaching qualification but it had been worth the effort. I had gained so much understanding of how a person learns, the different types of learners, motivation skills and, most importantly how little I actually knew about teaching, and that it was going to be a lifelong endeavour to learn as much as I could. If I was going to teach, then I was going to teach to the best of my ability. University for me had been fun. So many of my fellow students were in their twenties and so naïve it made me smile sometimes. It made me remember me at that age; I became a sounding board for ideas, a person to ask advice of. From them I got all the enthusiasm of youth. It was a good arrangement from which we all benefited. It certainly helped our group work to have such diversity.

As I have said the woman I was with had not seen the point of all the work and now the realisation that I would be doing a lot more work sank in. That was more or less the end of that relationship.

It was shortly afterwards that I heard Phil had split from his current girlfriend and was being pursued by credit card and poll tax debt collectors, among others and had moved out to an address that was harder to find. He was in fact living in a caravan he had rented from local farmer paying cash, and please don't ask for a receipt!

I had by now stopped looking for a church. They were all C of E or similar around where I was living, and, to be honest, I had stopped looking because in a way I was content to just read when I felt like it and didn't, I thought, need a church in my life. How wrong I was! Had I realised it then I might have saved myself some considerable heart ache and a lot of pain but I still didn't really believe that Satan truly existed. My girlfriend regarded what had happened in America as similar to a holiday romance, fantastic at the time but not for real life. She had also accepted Christ as her saviour when I did but her faith only lasted until we got home, or perhaps not even that long.

I kept my faith by reading my bible when the urge took me. I never doubted what had happened to me in America. I couldn't bring myself to put it down to imagination, I know how a bike behaves, and I can't fool myself into believing something different. It is the only way I could have been shown God's power. He did the impossible. I know what happened isn't possible so I can't deny it, or find another explanation for it. I either accept it as God's work or I say that I had been hallucinating? If I were to say that then what about the witnesses; did they also have the same hallucination? Where do we stop trying to find another answer to explain away what happened and just admit the truth, God is amazing!

Violence was still part of me. No matter how often I asked God to help me overcome it in my prayers they were never answered. I was deeply confused by what had happened to me. I knew what had happed on that mountain and in church later had been real, but why was I still so full of doubts?

Sometime later I found my 'science' reason for God in this world with the big bang theory. Who else can make everything from nothing? Science at last admitting it didn't have a complete answer for where we had come from, so God was real to me in everything I did. I knew he was with me, so why did I keep falling under Satan's power?

I had realised by now that was what was happening to me and that Satan didn't want to lose one of his disciples, something I had been all my life without knowing it. It was at this point, I think, I first started to admit I needed help and that as a solitary Christian I was and always would be at great risk of Satan grabbing me back.

That is the hardest part to see. When he has you there is no looking at yourself in honesty. It is always someone else's fault that you are how you are, that you act as you do. He takes pleasure in our torment and fights to keep you from Christ the Saviour. He blinds you to the truth.

That year Phil died. He had been having headaches for months but he didn't tell anyone.

The last time I saw him alive he had come to mine for a barby (barbecue) and got very drunk and was as happy as I can ever remember him being. He enjoyed a party, being full of stories and jokes; he was generally well liked because you could rely on his word.

He stayed that night and we talked into the small hours, drinking and sharing joints and of course raiding the fridge! We laughed about America, women, and life in general. His aches and pains, mine. Two bikers, reminiscing on times past and wishing we were twenty years younger.

He had no solid plans but I sensed he was tired of having nothing permanent in his life. He was talking about looking for a small farm and renting it so he could settle down and try and sort his life out.

He wanted to find some peace in his life and make a business buying and selling bike parts, something he had done before and was good at.

I promised I would 'keep an eye open for anything going in the North East'. I never got the chance.

The next day he set off home, we said our goodbyes and I watched him ride away; I listened as his engine noise faded into the distance.

I would never see him alive again.

I was at home when I heard he had been found dead in his caravan. There was nothing anyone could have done, he had suffered a brain haemorrhage in the night and his death had been very quick.

One sour point though, he had a multi tool, a good one made in America by 'Leatherman'. He always wore it, it never left his belt. I had admired it so much and so often that while we were in the USA I bought a similar one, I still have it. However when he was found by some of the men who rented units and vans on the same site the leather 'holster' was on his belt but the tool itself was missing. It has never been found. Draw your own conclusions. As far as I am concerned someone stole it from a dead man and that for me is about as low as it gets. When his time comes and he is judged how will he explain that theft?

When Phil was cremated I said goodbye to only the second true friend I had ever had. He wasn't perfect. Frankly some people never liked him because he could be 'blunt' to say the least at times. But, to me, he was loyal and trustworthy, something I hope he felt he could say about me. Don't misunderstand me here; he and I fell out a few times. We could both be stubborn. Neither liked admitting he was wrong. The bottom line though is I loved him like the brother I lost. I will never forget him or how much I valued his friendship. He left children from various relationships, some loved him some didn't, but they will all miss him even if they don't realise it for a few years. I believe the day will come when they look back, and see a guy who could be so wrong at times and so stubborn and stupid but who had a heart of gold and a generous caring and loving nature that so many took advantage of.

He once needed help to move and clear his house of all the rubbish and junk that had collected over the years. He asked about amongst all the people he had lent money to, stored their bikes for them for free, and helped them out in so many different ways. What happened, well they were all 'too busy' to be able to help, maybe next time. It fell to me and another mate to travel seventy five miles to help him. What a world, what a bunch of people in it. I hope when they look at themselves in the mirror one day and remember, I hope they see the truth of who they really are.

Phil had been in a major accident years before and had his hip joint replaced with a stainless steel one. I had promised him that if he went before me part of him would always ride with me. His hip joint now lives with me! I will keep it always, where I go it goes, as promised.

I had been back from the USA for five years and the relationship I was in was over. I was a lodger in my own house, separate rooms and no shared interests. The violence, the mistrust and lies from one or the other, it had all contributed to the inevitable breakdown but what was I to do? I knew I was never going to be happy there but why should anything else or anywhere else be any different?

I finally moved out, the plan being to eventually find a place of my own and live alone. It was preferable to going through another broken relationship with all the pain that generated. I was certain that mentally I couldn't stand it all again. I needed peace in my life and if it was living alone that gave it to me then so be it, no big deal, I had spent many years one way or the other alone. My major regret was that I was leaving behind several friends whom I had learned to trust and enjoyed being with. Many happy hours had been spent in my shed bike building or just passing time with a joint together. We were all also sea fishermen, out there on the ocean there is a peace found nowhere else. The friendship and natural camaraderie among six or eight guys on a fishing trip is only understandable to those who have been there. One friend I had known for twenty years or so, I had watched his family grow up, seen the hard times and the good times and yes I would miss his company. The other I had known for seven or eight years as a neighbour, by far the best neighbour I had ever known he too had become a good friend, but now I was leaving. I had two rooms that were mine, my bedroom and my study. And was, in some perverse way, if not content, I had at least learned to tolerate my situation and make the best of it. I know this may sound like the moans of someone who has given up but that is honestly how I felt at the time.

I did a lot of work at home so I spent a lot of time in my study with the computer. Maybe just surfing more often research for lessons I was due to deliver. Time passed.

I wrote a complete ten week 160 hour course during this period for delivery to young people with problems. I also wrote a manual handling course and a health and safety booklet for people with learning difficulties. I wrote several multiple choice test papers for pedestrian operated machinery training courses. I kept busy!

I prayed and I read my bible, not as much as I should have but enough to make me realise that without Jesus I had been living for no other reason than self-gratification in one form or another. I prayed so often for help. 'Dear God I want to change, please help me'. I never got an answer, or so I thought at the time. I tried to be a better person but there was still that feeling within me that I wasn't yet complete, that hollow that only Jesus can fill. What could I do? So, where was I at this point in my life? I was fifty seven years old. I had grown up abused and battered. My childhood had for the most part been a nightmare of fear and violence. I am left with both physical and mental scars. I had in turn become the abuser. I had been sexually assaulted. I had learned never to trust <u>any</u> woman; they are all liars and deceivers, I only used them, I never respected them. I had fully trusted only those two men other than my father. All now were deceased. I had been a drug addict and was still a drug user. Violence was still very much part of me. I was not a nice person. My life to this point had been lived for me. By that I mean I had done whatever would serve me the best, be it violence in a relationship, drug abuse, lies, theft, you name it I was up for it. So what had changed since that day on the mountain? I have said I will be honest in this account. Had anything really changed? Well, yes, everything and yet nothing. I knew God was real, I knew He had saved me. I didn't know why. I had changed inside but I still felt alone. I was so confused by it all. I went down on my knees begging for help many times. I was also still visiting the porn sites online and doing drugs, drinking myself into a stupor, swearing and living as I always had. As far as I could tell my life was the same as ever. To be blunt, the devil still ruled me and I was blind to the truth of my situation. I was full of doubt and confusion. Had there been other Christians for me to talk to then it would have become obvious what was wrong. I had been baptised in Spirit in America, I had taken Jesus as my saviour but I had not been baptised in water or repented my sins. More on this later, for now let's just say I was still very vulnerable to Satan and all his works. It was Satan that was doing his best to make me doubt the reality of what had happened to me. I knew Jesus was real but I didn't have the armour that God gives you when you have faith in Him. Gradually I was losing my battle with Satan without even knowing it. In time I would have gone back to being who I had been before America. Only now believing in God but having no faith in him to help me. I was, I believe like so many Christians, I believed in Jesus but I hadn't given him my life. I hadn't said 'I am Yours Lord, use me as you will' and meant it. To say that takes more than belief, it takes faith, complete faith in Christ Jesus that I didn't at this time have.

Across America, my Indian Chief 1300cc

Phil on his Indian Super Chief 1480cc

Roaming Europe, my V1100 fuel injected California

Off road fun, a tough little bike that would go anywhere.

Chapter 4. An Albanian mud Wrestler

A second beginning

There were the heavens and the earth and then the internet.

Sometimes when I had to have a break from lesson planning or research I would go to the various chat rooms. There are always new ones springing up. You never knew what the chat was going to be about unless you go to a subject specific site.

Usually it is wherever the chat goes it goes and I liked those because sometimes I would find someone either talking sense on a difficult subject or a nut. The only sites I found that were terminally boring were the pseudo community rooms where all you got were never ending E-Flirting, everyone pretending to be something they weren't, what a bunch of plonkers! Randy Wendy from Wickham says 'Hi to all my fans' oh please!

Conspiracy nuts are my favourite people on the web. I have heard all about how we never made it to the moon, that it was all done to fool the Russians, filmed here on earth somewhere out in the American desert. I have also read about the families who control all governments by their control of the money markets. I wonder if there may actually be some truth in this one. Both really interesting in their own way but, on balance, I think wrong. My favourite must be that the royal family are in fact reptiles from a previous age that got here via a time warp when their civilisation was destroyed by a giant meteor and changed their appearance to fool us all into thinking they are human. One day they will bring the rest of the reptiles through the time warp and conquer earth, you never know! Do you remember the X files? 'Somebody out there knows the truth'.

One night I happened on this 'partygal1' on one of the sites, I can't remember the name but I think I got there through 'Gum tree' or maybe not, who knows. I asked Kris and she doesn't remember either, not that it really matters now. I was always chatting to odd people; they are so much more interesting than so called 'normal' people. In this case it seemed about as it always was, someone expounding their personal theory about something, normally nothing to write home about but she (?) was going on about faith and what it meant to her. Looking back I realise now that God was at work in my life here. I have no doubts why my first conversation was about faith! The very thing I was lacking. I read for a while then had to send a reply telling her she was wrong and you can have faith in a mushroom. Some of the people I know do just that, so what! Didn't do you a lot of good though did it.

That did it! I won't repeat the discussion but we both enjoyed it and I found a friend who in that first meeting taught me more about what faith actually was than I had ever known. I found we both agreed about what we termed empty faith; in the end we swapped e-mail addresses. I told Kris about the problems I was having believing and all that had happened to me in Oregon. And how strong my belief in God was and why. She told me about her life and her faith and that she believed that God was always part of her life, in everything she did or said God was with her. He never let her down, never ignored her, even during her lowest times when she had ignored Him. He had been with her.

Now, I must give a word of warning here to all you reading this. Until that moment we had spoken anonymously, now we were taking that first step towards the real world as opposed to the cyber world where we had met. There we could be anything or anyone. In the real world we had to be ourselves. For some people this seems impossible, they cling to their cyber identities as if the deception wont in the end be discovered.

I remember watching a TV program where this very nice girl had been e-mailing a nice sounding guy, she was in the UK he was in Canada. He had come to meet her but he had been lying about himself.

She was waiting for a tall slim guy who's picture she had seen (his mate) and he was short and fat (okay then, weight challenged). The moment they met you could see the look of horror on her face, not what she had been expecting. The sad thing is, if he had been honest she may have liked him for himself, after all the only part of 'him' that was a deception was his physical appearance. It turned out that although he had been honest about his life and interests he had lied about his looks. As it was she was not happy about being lied to and he went home the next day, what a waste of time.

So beware, be honest.

Why do people lie to each other on the internet? 'Blond, blue-eyed and beautiful' turns out to be an Albanian mud wrestler called Igor looking for a date! What is the point? Stick to the truth, it is far, far, better in the long run in <u>any</u> situation.

As a Christian, however difficult, I always try to tell the truth. And yes, sometimes I fail. I am not and never will be perfect. I still have to say sorry to God more often than I would like. I am just so grateful that He always listens, and always forgives me.

Being honest

Another path in the road of life had just opened. God was at work. Kris could have been anywhere in the world, she was twenty minutes away.

From the very beginning she and I hit it off and were so happy to find that we were both Christians and both in need of a friend. We talked for a long time actually months via e-mail then arranged to meet.

At that moment she had my photo but I had never had one from her. This was a worry. So many times I had heard the stories about lonely wives looking for a good time with no commitments so I was quite concerned that either this was something like that or worse still 'she' was a guy! Remember the Albanian mud wrestler!

I got the photo just one hour before we were due to meet. She looked kind of shy, but lovely, yes disabled, yes overweight, but to me she looked fine but deeply troubled. Her eyes were dark shadows and she looked truly depressed like the weight of the world was upon her.

We had talked about every subject under the sun, and we had a rule, the truth, only the truth, and no matter what, the truth.

I had told her some of my life, she told me about hers. So I knew she was disabled and fighting her weight, she knew I was an ex addict and about the violence also that I was older than she was. We had talked about everything including all our likes and dislikes, our needs, our faults and fears, but I was unprepared for the deep sadness I saw in her in that first photograph.

We met in a pub car park in Durham. Two people who had become friends on the internet met in person for the first time, two lives that would never be the same again.

I drove into that car park afraid that she wouldn't want to even talk to me. Although I had said I had been honest about all things, I had in fact lied to her about my name.

Because of my work I had used my middle name to protect my identity when on the internet. I was worried by so many irrational fears, I later learned that she was feeling worse than I was and was afraid that I would just drive in and straight out when I saw her. I saw her car and pulled in, one car between us. She got out and I walked around my car to greet her 'hello I'm

Chris' was in my head, instead, without warning, I said 'Let's get this over with' and kissed her!

Shock from <u>both</u> of us, me for having done it I had <u>no</u> intention of doing anything but say hello and her for having responded! I cannot describe how I felt, what had I done...what a stupid thing to do...why? So much turmoil and confusion in my head I really expected to get my face slapped. To this day I am still amazed that I didn't. Kris said later that to anyone else she would have.

Not the plan at all. Well, not our plan anyway. We both looked at the other in shock did a sort of embarrassed 'er sorry' Hi I'm Chris and lets go in to the pub'. We sat at a table and talked, at first it was difficult but after only a few moments we felt like friends who were meeting again after a long break apart.

By then we both felt that God was guiding us something we had talked about via e-mail. We were later reminded of the bible passage where it says 'God brings the lonely together'. We both felt so close to each other from the very beginning, as if we had known each other for years. It is very odd to meet someone for the first time and to know more about them than some couples would know about each other after years together.

Since then God has done so very much for us.

Our rule still stands though. We never lie to each other, NEVER. No matter how painful we are always honest with each other. Kris knows and understands my lack of trust in women. She knew that first day that the quickest way to lose me was to lie to me.

The first year was the most difficult as we were both strong people and both needed to adapt a little to the other. However we never doubted that God had brought us together for a purpose, even in the beginning we had both felt that. Okay some would say it was all coincidences, perhaps some could be described that way but not all. There have been so many things that have happened to us that it's either God or the best run of

116

luck ever known to man and we should go to Vegas and win our fortune. It started with that chat about faith, and please remember Kris could have been anywhere in the world. Where was she? Twenty minutes down the road. Since then it's as if the road ahead of us was being planned and we were being guided. This suggests we don't have free will; I will come to that later but for now please except it is a very good feeling to have a guide on the road of life as we have, not to fear what's ahead.

We knew we needed God, or perhaps more accurately, we also needed to be with other Christians and to worship Him fully.

We tried a local country church, then a bigger Pentecostal church but I couldn't accept their doctrine. I have a science background and just can't bring myself to ignore all the evidence that shows the world to be older than the six thousand years they believe it to be. To all those Christians who do believe that, in the same way you can't believe in evolution I can't believe in that form of creationism, I still love Jesus with all my heart as I know you do, but we must disagree on how we interpret what the bible describes. I have no intention of getting stuck here in what is still a point of debate for many Christians. All I can say is this, does it really matter which way we believe God created us and all things? As long as we both agree that he did. Frankly, they didn't take too well to Kris arguing a point of doctrine with one of the elders either, and putting him in the position of either having to say that God made mistakes or that Kris was correct in her assertions. I should add at this point that I am also not a believer in random chance either. When you consider the human DNA chain to say it came about by chance is for me stretching the laws of probability a bit too far. If I must define my belief then I can only say that I believe the world and everything in it was made and is maintained by God. How I'm not sure, but I will continue to search for an answer that fits the facts as we know them and also fits with my certain knowledge of the existence of God.

I have said Kris and I felt so close to each other. After the first few months we both knew that we were meant to be together, we felt so right as though we had been together for years.

We were going to a different church together now and I was for the first time feeling at peace with my faith and my life. At last God was real for me and I was able to worship in the way I wanted to and raise my voice in praise to my saviour Jesus as I had in America when I was first saved.

It was about this time that Kris and I had decided to visit Holy Island. It was our first time away together and we had a very special reason for wanting to pray together in the church there.

This was to be a life changing visit for both of us.

We walked as far as Kris could that day which because of her disability was not very far. Then we sat in the car looking out over the sea and at the castle in the distance. It was a perfect scene. There is so much peace there on that island the presence of the Holy Spirit is so strong everywhere.

It is no surprise that Christianity grew strongly here as it spread out into the surrounding countryside; St Cuthbert was carried to Durham where he is now buried by the monks from Holy Island which is also known as Lindisfarne. There are so many wonderful stories linked to this island, so much peace, sometimes it is difficult to remember how old Christianity is here.

We drove down into the main village to the church there. A raw wind blows across the grave yard from the sea smelling of salt and seaweed reminding you that this is an island, continually assaulted by the harsh weather in winter, a difficult place to have chosen to live and build on. There is power and presence there, standing in that small church I knew God was watching and listening. I knew He was with us. For us then, in that place, our lives had reached a turning point from which, for us, there could never be any turning back. We were there to talk to God and to ask a question. Why there and not in any other place? Well for both of us it felt as though we had to do it there, that's all I can say about that, it wasn't really our choice. We had been led to this place at this time. Since then this 'having to go somewhere' has led us around the world to countries we had never dreamed of visiting. We believe God is going to use us, if he calls then we obey without question or hesitation. However, that is for later, for now, back to Holy Island on that cold windswept day.

Our relationship had reached the point where we were certain of our love and of our great need to be together, but were both uncomfortable about a physical relationship and I do know that seems odd for me but I had changed from who I had been. We both believed strongly in scripture and that we should be married before that happened.

Our prayer and a new person is born

We knelt in that small church there before God and asked Him to bless our love and said that we wanted to be together now and for always as man and wife. We made a vow that day to God. We realised then as we do now that some people will feel this was a 'cop out' just a way to satisfy our lust and had very little to do with the love we felt for each other or our faith. In effect a way of justifying our living together. We prayed for guidance. To tell us if what we were doing was in His eyes wrong to judge us as our Lord and Saviour and to give us either guilt or joy, for Him to look into our hearts and see the truth that was there.

I was reminded recently of the custom of early American settlers who wanted to marry but no preacher was available. They would gain the approval of their parents and live together as man and wife before God until the travelling preacher passed through. Then they would make their union 'official' in the eyes of the church and the law. Yes, we could have gone to a registry office but to us that would have been meaningless, a gesture nothing more. What we did that day was to swear to our God and ask his blessing. We knew that day we had married in the eyes of the Lord, but not we knew in the eyes of man.

For us, from that day we have been man and wife. The date we celebrate as our wedding anniversary when we were first joined is the 8th of October.

The law of man may not agree but our Lord is higher than any mortal law. We believe very strongly 'whom God hath joined together let no man put asunder'. We were joined in the eyes of God that day and we both felt so full of joy as we left there. We knew that we would never be alone again and that we would always have each other and our saviour.

Kris moved in with me and we were living as a married couple and were both very happy. At times my past still interfered with our lives. I still had huge problems with trust but little by little I was getting better. Kris understood and helped me so much. We prayed together for help and salvation.

We were going to church together regularly and I had decided that despite being married on Holy island I wanted to marry Kris and make her my wife in the eyes of society and the law, before witnesses and our church.

I knew I couldn't ask her until I had put my past behind me. I was still the same person as I had always been. Yes I had my faith in Jesus to help me but as yet I had not fully given myself to him. I wanted to leave my sinful past and come fully into the light of His love. It was important to me that my friends and all who knew me realised that I, as they had known me was gone forever. I wanted to arrange that my name, Reginald, the person I didn't want to ever be again was lost. I did this by deed poll, taking the name I was known by now, my middle name as my first name.

I kept Reg as it was my father's name as my middle name, out of respect and love for him. I arranged for this to become legal on the same date that I was to be baptised. I had asked to be baptized some weeks earlier and the date had been set.

It says in the bible, *Jesus said, 'Truly, truly, I say to you, unless one is born again he cannot see the kingdom of God'*. John chapter 3 verse 3. Baptism is an outward sign of that rebirth. We, in my church believe that the only way to be baptised is by full immersion in water, as it was done in the time of Jesus. Later in John, Jesus say's *'Truly, truly, I say to you, unless one is born of water and the Spirit, he cannot enter the kingdom of God'*. John chapter 3 verse 5.

My baptism in water took place in the River Wear before witnesses from my church and non-Christian friends. I gave my life to Christ and repented all my sins on the 5th of September 2010. When I came out of that water I truly was, 'born again', a new creation. Reginald was gone, Christopher was born.

Some 'friends' can't accept the change and want to ignore what I have done. I have also lost some friends who see me now as someone a bit weird. It is a shame FOR THEM that they can't cope with my love for Jesus. I wish they could, so many other friends have accepted my choice, they may not agree, or even understand but they respect my decision. I must point out that for every 'friend' I have lost I have gained at least ten who love me for who I am now!

For three days and two nights I didn't sleep, I was burning almost like a fever, no sweat just hot, full of energy from the Holy Spirit bubbling through me. To be completely honest, the last time I had felt like this was when I was doing fet, (amphetamine sulphate) only this was much much better.

I read my bible, walked about the house thinking, knelt in prayer, laid down in pointless attempts to sleep.

Then finally on the third day I slept. Fourteen hours, later I awoke refreshed and into the worst battle I have ever had with Satan, a battle that tested my faith to its limit.

If I ever had any doubt that he was real then this ended that doubt forever.

Satan, Beelzebub, the devil

Satan is REAL and he is EVIL and he is OPPOSED to Jesus Christ our saviour and all he stands for. If Christ is a great light then Satan is a pit of endless dark.

If we as mortals ever give him complete dominion over us then we are lost to the fires of hell. Remember that, we have to give him dominion; we have to make that choice, he can't make us.

It seems fashionable now to deny that Satan exists and that all man's troubles are his and his alone, but if we deny Satan then we must also deny God, heaven and the very concept of a hell.

I have many questions and very few answers. I am not trying to say I understand God's plan, nobody can, but He gave me an inquiring mind so I will use it as I always have, to inquire, to search, to try and gain an insight into the truth. I have said many times that I have no problem with God having a plan for me, I just wish He would show me a little more of it.

I have been so blessed by God. When I doubted and would not believe He showed me the truth of His existence in a way I couldn't ignore. In the same way He let me see the power of Satan, not as an abstract thought but as a real threat to me, my life and my love of Jesus. Without the help of Kris who prayed with me and stood by my side, without my saviour Jesus who was always there to give us the strength to resist, I might have lost my faith in the next two days and returned to being a disciple of the devil. This was the last real chance he had to get me back; he came close but failed, as he always will as long as we give him no dominion over us. And now I know I never shall.

If you have read this far then you know that I had been a disciple of the devil, in my ignorance, all my life, until I took Christ Jesus as my saviour and my eyes were opened.

I awoke.

My first thought was I wanted a joint, what was the point, why was I bothering? I needed my drugs.

It was all bullshit, I could never change, why would I want to?

I remember telling Kris that she and I was a huge mistake and that I didn't love her or want to be with her, that I wanted her out of my life. As far as I was concerned Jesus and the whole lot of you could go screw, it wasn't for me and never would be.

No way was I ever going to surrender myself to some invisible spirit and let my life be directed by what I said, at the time, was a joke. I wanted no part of it, not now, not ever.

I was never going to be anything other than in charge of my own life. I was the driver and I was never going to allow some superstition to rule me.

Church was a fantasy for the weak minded that I was never going to go back to. How the f#ck I had ever been conned into being baptised was a mystery, it was nothing, it was a complete con.

Kris, God bless her, held onto her love for me and prayed for me, I refused to even consider prayer.

This went on for hours. Shouting and abuse from me but thank God no violence, understanding and help from Kris. How she put up with it I don't know. I was back to being nearly the guy I had been for years when I was with the worst of the bike clubs. I had no respect for Kris and I repeatedly told her to f#ck off out of my life and let me be who I really was. All I wanted was to get my bike out, pack my stuff and p#ss off back to my bro's and a decent life again.

Why had she screwed up my life, why had I ever allowed her to con me into all this bullshit?

Finally I told her to get out of my sight and I went to bed, sleeping in my office our front bedroom on a duvet on the floor. I was so full of anger that it took ages for me to get to sleep; there was also a degree of guilt about how I had spoken to Kris that I denied feeling. The nightmares were awful, full of violence and hate, scenes that brought out the very worst of me.

Morning came, I don't remember what time I finally got up but I know it was early. Kris was exhausted but she got up and we tried to talk, not very successfully as I was still adamant that I was leaving and as soon as I could find somewhere I was away and gone from her, from church and from God.

I now know that she prayed for me repeatedly and never gave up on me. Finally after another day of me abusing Kris, telling her it was over and I was leaving as soon as I could and still refusing to pray I went to bed.

There alone in the quiet I knew Jesus was still with me, questioning what I was doing, asking me why? That still small voice in the darkness of my night. At last I finally admitted to myself that I was wrong. It seemed so hard to admit this but I knew I was being held back from telling Kris I needed her and Christ. And in addition to that I was afraid in case Kris told me she didn't want me anymore, Satan again this time whispering and poring doubt into my ear.

For a long time I lay there trying to move but not being able to, so afraid to. I know that sounds weird but it is the truth, it was as though despite wanting to, I couldn't move. The room was so dark, a thick darkness through which I was afraid to reach out and find the light switch, I was afraid of touching something there in the dark. Something I knew was there, a presence, real and cold, I could sense the evil from it. This may be hard to grasp but it was like a black light. Not a light that gives illumination but one that hides everything in its darkness.

Finally I managed to find the courage to get up and went to Kris and asked her to help me. To be honest I begged her. I told her I didn't know what was happening to me and that I was so afraid that I was going back to who I had been. She said she knew and had been praying for me and that she had been afraid as well but believed that Jesus was with us and would help me if I would let Him. We talked and prayed for hours, she was so understanding and explained quietly what she believed was happening to me.

She had once told me that Satan would challenge me if I was ever baptised because by so doing we stand out from the crowd. I tell people now that if you look at a flock of sheep and one puts its head up which do you look at?

It's like that with Satan. He sees you now standing out from the flock and will try to destroy all that is happening to you, all you are doing to move away from him and to the love of Christ, if he can. If you let him he will succeed but you and only you can allow him to have you. He cannot force you; you have dominion over him, not the other way around.

Finally, praying together, we told Satan again and again he had no dominion over me, Kris or our lives and never would. We denied him and commanded him to leave me alone. 'I would never again be his or walk the path he had once laid out for me' that sounded so easy to say but it wasn't, it took hours to reach this point and a lot of crying, stress and prayer from both of us.

I asked forgiveness for all I had said and done of Jesus, and that he would forever be with me to help me overcome any further attacks from Satan. We prayed for a long time until we knew I was free and Satan defeated, driven from us.

I know that to you that may sound so strange, but for me and any other Christian it is simple. Satan will offer you the world, as he did for Jesus, he will threaten you, trick you, anything to keep you and it isn't until you are free of him that you can truly see what he has been doing in your own life. How he has been deceiving you. Satan is not the horned cloven hoofed devil depicted in some paintings or illustrations. At least we don't see him that way. Satan is that money lender, that nice guy in a suit who offers you a deal you can't refuse. The get rich quick money making scheme or the voice in your head that tells you 'do it, you can get away with it'. Think, if Satan was that horned beast would anyone be tempted by him? Would anyone trust him? He is above all not stupid and he knows your weaknesses, and will act on that knowledge to your detriment. If for one moment you think you are immune to him then beware, he is closer than you can possibly know. His hand is on your shoulder.

Kris and I are so strong together; more than just the two of us, there is also Christ with us, guarding us, protecting us, giving us his armour, armour that you too can have. Together we drove Satan out never to return, never to have me as his disciple again, never to lead me in ignorance and darkness, never again to be my master. I know you now Satan, I can see you, it is over; I refuse to give you dominion over me ever again.

I am now a true disciple of Christ. I have lived as a chattel of the devil, walked his path, even praised him and exalted him, but never again. My eyes are open to his deceitful evil ways now, I am free of his influence, free of his malevolent presence forever.

Dear reader, if you love Christ then you know how I felt after we had prayed and I was free. If you don't yet know the joy of his love, then I beg you go and find help because Satan has many ways to deceive you into thinking all is well. You may be going to church, you may believe yourself free of sin, but are you? If you haven't taken Christ as your saviour then all I can say to you is 'all is not well' and you are being deceived. Please open your eyes.

Ask yourself, are you happy? Truly at peace within yourself, free of sin? Could you face death and say honestly that you are not afraid to meet your maker, to answer for your life? For all your deeds and for all your sins left un-repented?

Remember the devil will walk with you right up to the point of your death, telling you all is well, after that you are on your own. What will you say to your saviour when you are judged? 'I meant to do something about it' or 'I was too busy' what is your excuse, what will you say? What will save you from hell? Okay, so you don't believe in hell, but I know it is real, as real as heaven, but I don't suppose you believe in that either do you?

I was like you once; I knew there was no God. I knew science was the only way. I couldn't believe that this entire world and this entire universe came about other than by some huge coincidental chance. Please believe me if I could save you I would, but I can't, only you can do that, through Christ our saviour, I pray you will. I pray this account of my life helps you to do that before it is too late for you. Before you are judged.

Forgiveness

This for any Christian is a must, but for many like me it is so difficult.

To forgive those that have sinned against you and by doing so to be free of the hate and anger is essential for you to be truly free of sin yourself, for not to forgive is a sin.

During my life I have been hurt by a lot of different people and have hurt many others myself. At the time I regarded it all as just part of life, now however I know I was wrong and in my heart I have forgiven almost all those who hurt me or wished me ill.

One part of forgiveness that I have trouble with is how to forgive myself for all the hurt I have done to others throughout my life. I try and can forgive myself most things I have done, but some things have been more difficult than others.

Forgiveness of my mother, that is so hard for me to do. I try and I have prayed for help, and yes I say 'I have forgiven her' but in my heart I have always known that isn't entirely true. She did me so much harm and has caused me and so many others, so much grief throughout my life that I thought I would never be able to forgive her completely.

Recently though in church I was prayed for to help me to forgive her. I feel that now maybe the time I finally can let go of the hate and really forgive. Why now, I really don't know it just feels right so since I was prayed for I have tried to remember to say 'I forgive you for all you did' every time I think of her. It's not easy but I am trying and with the help of Jesus I know I will succeed and then I will have taken another small step towards living as Kris and I want to, that is by the scriptures.

The other great problem I have is Fred. What happened there has coloured my attitude to sex offenders all my life, even now I cannot forgive him although I know I should. As I have said before in this account I am far from perfect but I am trying.

I will seek help from my church elders on this point and ask for prayer to help me come closer to Jesus and how he wants us all to live. I know in time with the help of my saviour I will overcome this hatred within me and be able to find forgiveness in my heart even for Fred.

I knew before I could ask Kris to marry me I had to tell her my story. I had told her so much but now I believed Jesus was telling me to tell her my entire life story all of it.

I thought the reason was that I never wanted anyone to say "did you know" and Kris not to be able to answer "of course I did", we have to be, and always will be, honest with each other. It is part of our strength. Perhaps though part of the reason was so that she would encourage me to write this account of my life, I know that without her support I wouldn't have. God is in control so only he knows all the truth.

So how do I go on from here?

As long as I know that Christ has forgiven me, and that I will always try to forgive others, then I know I will be okay. I know he understands my weaknesses and imperfections and forgives me. Every day I ask for and am granted that forgiveness for all my sins. Jesus died on the cross for me just so I could say that and know it is the truth. Through him and only through him I am free of my sin because he took it upon himself that day on the cross.

Home

Time passes as it does and Kris and I got happier and happier, finally I asked her to formally marry me.

Why did I want to marry Kris in this way? After all the pain marriage has given in the past? It is perhaps hard for you if you are a non-Christian to understand. Since I have been baptised the word of God, the bible, has become real to me. Within it are the teachings and laws of our God. One of those laws is that we must be married before we make love together.

Despite our oath to God and our belief that we married on Holy Island I felt that we should be joined together in our church by an elder, before witnesses and before God.

Let marriage be held in honour among all, and let the marriage bed be undefiled, for God will judge the sexually immoral and adulterous.

Hebrew 13 verse 4.

I don't mean I am in fear of breaking that law, I mean it is a joy to obey it. So what had once been something to avoid at all costs now became a wonderful gift.

We had already asked God to bless our union and looking back we believe he had. But, as I have said I wanted to make it official, in law and in front of our brothers and sisters.

Now I know that for some this is a difficult concept but to us it really is simple. We were joined before God at Holy Island. We believe we were married in His eyes from that moment on. Yet we both felt that we should 'marry' in front of our church. Why? One reason in all honesty was to satisfy society. The main reason however was to be joined <u>publicly</u> before our God in front of our friends and brothers and sisters, and to celebrate that joining in our church. So for us now we have two dates to celebrate. I know that for some Christians this explanation won't do and they will go on believing we weren't married until we were joined in church on the 14th May 2011. So be it. God knows the truth.

I really couldn't believe I had done it, I had been thinking about it for months, I had got the ring (sized by feeling her finger as we held hands) and knew what I was going to say.

Maybe I am a bit old fashioned but I believe it is up to the man to choose the engagement ring. To offer the engagement ring as a 'Fait accompli' to his 'intended', 'I offer this as a sign of our betrothal'.

The ring I chose has three diamonds; each diamond represents a part of our relationship, our love, our faith and our absolute honesty with each other.

Our relationship is like a tripod, one leg cannot stand without the other two, each leg is as vital as the other. We are like that - without our love, our faith and our honesty we couldn't be together and be so happy.

I knelt and asked if she would do me the honour of becoming my wife, she said "yes, oh yes".

We were married in our church by our senior elder, in front of all our church family and friends; it was a great day of joy and happiness for all concerned. About 130 adults and 40 children came, wonderful.

We had balloons, flags and squeakers for the children as we wanted them to have fun and to celebrate our joining before God and the making of our union legal in the eyes of the state. They were as much a part of our wedding as anyone else.

We didn't want parents having to tell their children to be quiet and behave, we absolved them of all responsibility for their children's behaviour and it worked. They were all so well behaved but involved and having fun.

It was exactly as Kris and I had wanted it to be. Everybody enjoyed themselves. It was a celebration, alive and full of joy but also deeply moving.

Tim was my best man. He is the son of Phil, he is a fine young man who has also had his share of problems with drugs and no doubt will have more.

I will do what I can for him. He knows how I felt about his father and that he can call on me at any time and I will be there for him. One day I hope to bring him to the love of Christ. We talk now and again and he visits Kris and me but not often enough as it isn't easy for him living so far away from here.

I pray one day he will walk with Christ.

Married life

Kris and I honeymooned in Italy and Albania it was there in Albania that we saw a country that needs Christ so much. The people are proud and friendly, always willing to help a stranger. The country is so very far behind the rest of Europe in its development as a nation because it had been cut off for many years by its communist government, now thankfully done away with.

Those people we talked to about our faith said 'Albania is our faith'! And so it has been for many years as with each new invader there came a new religion. The Albanians adopted the attitude that as long as they have Albania then faith or religious belief doesn't really matter. A Muslim said to me 'my father is Muslim; my grandfather was a Jew, what am I? I don't go to the mosque but my friends call me Muslim! I am just an Albanian what else is there'. I said there is Christ, but he didn't understand what I meant. We came home feeling so different to how we felt when we left.

At our wedding I said the difference for two Christians when they marry is that there can never be divorce, other than for adultery.

A man shall leave his father and his mother and hold fast to his wife, and the two shall become one flesh. So they are no longer two but one flesh. What therefore God has joined together let no man separate.

Matthew 19 verses 5 and 6.

We have made an oath to God and yes we feel different because of that, but it is so much more than that. How can I explain how it feels to be in love with two 'people' at the same time, but I am and so is Kris, it is wonderful. It is like nothing I have ever felt before.

As I sit writing this at the computer my wife is behind me in the same room painting, with the TV on in the background. We are both so in love and so very happy in our marriage not only to each other but also to Jesus who has saved us both. There are three in this marriage, a triangle of love.

Where my life is going now I don't know, however I will never be alone again and neither will Kris. Christ Jesus walks with us both.

We both feel God has a task for us; we are His to do with as he wills, we are His disciples and his willing servants. Every day we thank God for bringing us together and pray that He is always at our side and in our marriage with us. I thank God every day for saving me and for washing away my sins. For making me anew.

I try every day to be totally open to His word and to live by the scriptures. Every day I fail and ask his forgiveness and that He helps me try again.

I know He understands me and knows that I will always fail but he blesses me for trying.

The Scriptures

I have mentioned 'the scriptures' several times in this account without explaining either what they are, or how important they are to me as a Christian.

Noun.

'Sacred writings of Christianity contained in the bible Or Passages of scripture the fundamental teachings of the scriptures'
Oxford English dictionary.

To me, this really just means 'the sacred word of God' written in the bible. It is the law I try to live by and my guide for all occasions. Some people will disagree with that statement and say that we don't have to obey all of God's laws. They will say that we can reinterpret those laws to suit modern society. Change them to allow for more liberal thinking, a more flexible way to look at right and wrong.

Are the Ten Commandments as given to Moses in the old testament of the bible still relevant?

"I am the LORD your God, which have brought you out of the land of Egypt, out of the house of bondage. You shall have no other gods before me.

You shall not make for yourself a carved image, or any likeness of anything that is in heaven above, or that is in the earth beneath, or that is in the water under the earth. You shall not bow down to them or serve them, for I the LORD your God am a jealous God, visiting the iniquity of the fathers on the children to the third and the fourth generation of those who hate me, but showing steadfast love to thousands of those who love me and keep my commandments.

You shall not take the name of the LORD your God in vain, for the LORD will not hold him guiltless who takes his name in vain.

Remember the Sabbath day, to keep it holy. Six days you shall labour, and do all your work, but the seventh day is a Sabbath to the LORD your God. On it you shall not do any work, you, or your son, or your daughter, your male servant, or your female servant, or your livestock, or the sojourner who is within your gates. For in six days the LORD made heaven and earth, the sea, and all that is in them, and rested on the seventh day. Therefore the LORD blessed the Sabbath day and made it holy.

Honour your father and your mother that your days may be long in the land that the LORD your God is giving you

You shall not murder.

You shall not commit adultery.

You shall not steal.

You shall not bear false witness against your neighbour.

You shall not covet your neighbour's house; you shall not covet your neighbour's wife, or his male servant, or his female servant, or his ox, or his donkey, or anything that is your neighbour's."

Exodus Chapter 20 verses 4-17

Some will say that these are laws given to the Jews in ancient times and are not meant for us in this enlightened day and age. I disagree; I believe that as a guide to life you cannot do better than to begin by obeying these laws. Scripture is my guide and my joy. Reading it has given me understanding where there was ignorance, clarity where there was confusion.

Before I was a Christian I had views that I cannot hold now. The way I look at life and the way I conduct myself has changed. An example is my changed view on homosexuality. For many years I believed that as long as you did no harm then do what you want to. This included homosexuality.

I had a bi-sexual friend, Gerry. He was a male stripper and spent a lot of his time in the gym working out. He had shoulder length blond wavy hair, stood six feet tall. The ladies loved him. He performed as 'Thor' on stage with a large hammer, a shield and very little else. He was very popular in gay clubs and bars. Many times I would go with him to 'watch his back' as some people after a drink or two could forget he was a performer and become a little too attentive. It was my job to gently dissuade them and get us out safely to the car.

I was comfortable in the company of homosexuals, I'm straight and they are gay, so what? Well since I became a Christian my view has changed.

'Or do you not know that the unrighteous will not inherit the kingdom of God? Do not be deceived: neither the sexually immoral, nor idolaters, nor adulterers, nor men who practice homosexuality, nor thieves, nor the greedy, nor drunkards, nor revilers, nor swindlers will inherit the kingdom of God'.

1 Corinthians Chapter 6 verses 9-10

This wasn't a conscious choice, I didn't wake one day and say 'homosexuality, adultery, theft or greed is a sin'. I did realise one day though that my view had changed, I don't know when exactly but it had. This is why I now believe that the church and all Christians should stand up against laws that would compel us to marry homosexual couples in our churches. As Christians we must say 'no, the law of God forbids it so we cannot.' The higher law must prevail. Not all Christians will agree however. I am not homophobic, but I do believe now that the act of homosexuality is a sin, as is stealing or adultery and only through the love of Jesus Christ can a person be forgiven their sins and enter the kingdom of heaven. I know many Christians will have different views, but I will continue to be guided by God's word.

My life has changed in so many ways since I became a Christian. I don't want to get into all the rights and wrongs of our society here that is not the purpose of this account. I will however say this. I believe that if we were truly a Christian society, and followed the teachings of God as detailed in the scriptures, then we would not have the massive problems we have in our society now. Look at any part of our society, from our politicians down to the homeless and unemployed, now tell me if our society isn't rotten and corrupt. Everywhere there is selfishness, lies, and abuse, look out for your own and never worry about the rest. Where is God in these lives, what has happened to us? When I talk to people about their views I seem so often to have the impression that they think they don't have to worry about death yet. That in some way they can 'sort it out tomorrow' I beg you to beware dear reader tomorrow may be sooner than you think. Sometimes I feel that Christians are like islands of hope in a sea of despair. We must become continents; we must encompass the world and drain those seas of despair with the love of Christ. We must stand up for our beliefs and our faith, and not be afraid, if that makes us unpopular, or brings us into conflict with the laws of this land then so be it. It won't be the first time. Christ Jesus is with us.

I truly believe, as long as we are true to the teachings of Jesus as detailed in the bible and have faith, we will overcome.

Going down...

Free at last! Reborn. My baptism in the river Wear 2010.

September 2010, no longer alone, Christ Jesus is by my side now and forever more. My life will never be the same again, thank God. I was his lost sheep but he came and found me because he loves me and wants me.

Chapter 5. Just Paddling along

The present day

God continues to work in my life. I am now on a voyage of discovery. Every day God gives me new reasons to be awed by His power. Every day I am humbled before him.

When I was baptised in Spirit in the USA and the Holy Spirit flowed into me, it felt like a flood entering me. Since then I have felt that flood again and again as I have been prayed over.

I have prayed for others and have seen the power of the Holy Spirit work through me and in them. I have seen miracles happen. I am a different person, the violence has gone. The mistrust I have always felt is beginning to ebb away. I know that all women are not the same and that most can be trusted. I don't smoke now, I don't use drugs. I try not to swear, I try to live as a good husband, by the scriptures, and bring only joy and pride to my wife. I honour her above all others. We both honour and love the lord.

I have recounted my experiences after my baptism in the river and how hard the fight with Satan was, but I have not mentioned the gifts that the Spirit will give.

The Bible tells us,

Now concerning spiritual gifts, brothers, I do not want you to be uninformed. You know that when you were pagans you were led astray to mute idols, however you were led. Therefore I want you to understand that no one speaking in the Spirit of God ever says "Jesus is accursed!" and no one can say "Jesus is Lord" except in the Holy Spirit. Now there are varieties of gifts, but the same Spirit; and there are varieties of service, but the same Lord; and there are varieties of activities, but it is the same God who empowers them all in everyone.   To each is given the manifestation of the Spirit for the common good. For to one is given through the Spirit the utterance of wisdom, and to another the utterance of knowledge according to the same Spirit, to another faith by the same Spirit, to another gifts of healing by the one Spirit, to another the working of miracles, to another prophecy, to another the ability to distinguish between spirits, to another various kinds of tongues, to another the interpretation of tongues. All these are empowered by one and the same Spirit, who apportions to each one individually as he wills.

For just as the body is one and has many members, and all the members of the body, though many are one body, so it is with Christ.

1 Corinthians Chapter 12, verses 4-12

The bible is quite clear on this. ALL Christians are given gifts by the Holy Spirit; it is what we do with this gift that is so very important.

If ignored, then Christ, I believe through the Holy Spirit, will remove them for a time. If however you use the gift in faith, then you will be granted more. By this I mean if I use a gift in faith then I will get better at it. Remember though, you are not doing anything; you are the tool God is using. You are His instrument. Be open to him and he will use you.

What I am going to relate to you now are my experiences since I was baptised. This is not a list of what you can expect and must not be considered as a guide to Christian gifts. It is what has happened to me. It is what I have been given by the grace of God. Many Christians have different gifts; many can use them more effectively than I do. I am far from being able to understand all that has happened to me since the day of my baptism, I am open to God and as time goes on I hope and pray that He will use me more and more often. I am His instrument; He will use me as He will.

I am truly blessed by God; He has allowed me through the Holy Spirit to heal. To be able to help the sick or those in pain even a little awes me.

I 'see' visions; sometimes as I pray, other times they can come without warning, mostly during song in church while I am praising God. Please understand, they are rare and few but very real when they happen, I know for non-Christians this may be hard to get hold of but for a Christian it is so simple to understand.

Finally, I have the strongest feeling that I have to preach, I don't know why, or where, I wish I did know but I have to. It is not something I would have chosen in the beginning, but the feeling is almost a need, so I will do my best, I have no choice.

I have given my life to Christ, He steers for me now, and I go where He takes me. I do what He asks of me.

I tell friends that my life is like a small boat on the ocean, Jesus is with me steering as I and Kris paddle. Sometimes the weather is bad and we struggle, at other times it is fine and pleasant and we go along without a care in the world. It is at these times that I have to remind myself that Jesus is with me and this time of easy passage will not last. At one time that thought would have been abhorrent to me, now there is comfort and joy in it.

Some weeks ago I preached for the first time in my church, my subject, miracles and do they still happen. I used as an example my wife and how through the work of Jesus she can now walk and is a living proof to his working of miracles amongst us.

I don't know if I will preach again. I think I will as I have things in me I want to say. I believe I can serve God by speaking of his greatness and love for all his children. My life has been what the Chinese would call 'interesting' I refer to the Chinese curse 'may you live in interesting times'. If I can tell others about my life, and that telling can contribute to someone being saved, then all the suffering will have been worth it.

Healing and the laying on of hands

I have already written about Kris and her disability. When we first met she could only walk using crutches and then with difficulty.

One of the conversations we had was to make sure I understood that before long I would be pushing her in a wheel chair. She wanted me to fully realise what I was taking on by staying with her. To quote her, 'I don't want a carer' strong woman my Kris, definitely a half full type.

She has progressive degenerative osteo arthritis with an exaggerated kyphosis and spondylitis of the spine.

Let me translate. She has arthritis in her joints, and a bent and fused spine that is crumbling.

There is x ray evidence of this, and it is all documented in her medical records. That, I think, is very important.

These are illnesses for which there is no cure; her condition can only become worse, her spine, more and more bent, her walking more and more difficult until she has to use a wheel chair. So says medical science.

When Kris and I pray for her to be healed I lay my right hand on the area we are concentrating on. If she is having bad hip pain, then that is where we concentrate.

When we first started doing this I asked Kris to describe what she was feeling. I did NOT tell her what I was feeling or my impression of what was happening. I wanted to be sure in, my own mind, that this wasn't self-delusion. If Kris felt the same as I did then it had to be real and not suggested by either of us.

I will describe what I and Kris feel during healing but please remember this is what WE feel and should not be taken as the template or model for anyone else. We all do what we do in our own way; the only common factor is God and His love for all of us.

We start by asking for God's help in what we are doing, by praying. Kris lays relaxed and I very gently put my right hand on the area of pain and my left hand on another area of her body. It doesn't seem to matter where, but by so doing it seems to make it easier for me to allow the Spirit to work in us.

Usually I just hold her hand. I always think of the flow of the Holy Spirit as if it was a waterfall landing on my head and from there down my arm to Kris. She feels it as do I as a tingling heat that grows stronger as we continue; this has on occasion become so strong that Kris has pulled away as it was 'too hot'. My arm always aches at the elbow afterwards and Kris feels numbness in the area we have been concentrating on.

What is happening? I don't know, I do however believe that through the action of the Holy Spirit healing is taking place. This, over time, has become evident by the improvement in Kris's condition.

We have prayed many times to reduce the pain and repair the damage in Kris and Jesus has been there with us. Our brothers and sisters from our Church have also prayed for her. There is great power in prayer, and Kris is being cured. I should explain for the non-Christian reader. When you become a Christian you join the family of God. He is the father, we are His children. We are all brothers and sisters in His family. What father would not help his children if they asked?

As I have said, when Kris and I first met she couldn't walk without crutches.

However, over the last year she has thrown away those crutches! She has gone from being unable to walk more than a few steps to only using a stick now for balance and she is now walking very much further.

She walked unaided at our wedding in high heeled shoes not using sticks all day. She can turn her head from side to side, turn at the hip, which incidentally has been impossible for her since her disease progressed into her spine and hip joints.

Remember, medical science says this cannot happen.

Now, some of her family who came to our wedding would attribute this improvement to having found a good man and being happy.

Well yes, maybe Kris has lost some weight, maybe she is walking better, because she is happier, but how do they explain that her spine has straightened and she has grown 1 ½ inches, okay I may be good but not that good!

She has had to buy adjustable sticks because she just keeps getting taller.

Each day she is improving, each day her spine becomes straighter. This cannot happen, medical science says this is impossible, a fused spine cannot straighten. However it has.

We believe that through prayer and the power of our faith in God through Jesus Christ she will continue to improve. That is our prayer and our belief.

Because of her improvement she is now fit enough to have an operation to replace one of her knees, an operation she couldn't have had a year ago simply because it wasn't worth it if she was going into a wheelchair.

By man's hand guided by God, or by God himself, Kris is getting better day by day.

I have said it many times and I know some Christians would not agree with me but I firmly believe that God helps those who help themselves.

Don't sit passively waiting for a miracle to cure you, act, pray, and above all have faith.

Yes I admit it would be spectacular if Kris was totally healed in one go, all her pain gone, fit and healthy.

Why hasn't God done just that? Why if God can heal hasn't He healed Kris in one burst instead of bit by bit?

I don't know the answer to that question, it's that simple. No matter how I try I can't understand God or His plan for us. Why He does what He does will remain a mystery to me until I pass from this world. Then, oh yes, then I will have a long list of questions for Him!

Then perhaps He will give me the understanding I crave, until that time all I can say is praise God and thank you for all you have done for Kris so far.

I was at a Christian convention recently and a lady who was partly blind and needed glasses was asked to lay her own hands on her eyes by a preacher and ask for healing, this she did and now doesn't need glasses. She has sight as good as anyone, she can read a test board when the moment before she couldn't. Before this is claimed as God's work she will be examined by an optician and the change authenticated. As with any healing it must be able to be shown to have actually happened and made a change that was not there before.

I believe in healing by the power of the Holy Spirit, most of my life I thought it was self-delusion or at best psychic energy, I was wrong. I have been wrong about a lot of things in my life. I am only now realizing just how wrong I have been about so much.

Visions and God speaking

Not so many years ago if someone had come to me and said 'I had a vision, I saw an angel' I would have been really impressed and wanted to know what drug they were on.

LSD has over the years been responsible for many weird and wonderful experiences; thankfully it was not a drug I ever tried.

I saw someone lose their career because of it so I stayed well away.

It was back in the early 70's. I know people always say the 60's were the best but for me it would have to be the 70's. There was still that feeling of change happening in the world, the belief that we, as young people, could really make a difference as I believe we did, that war, hate, prejudice could all be swept away by love. In many ways it was a spiritual time, very often misguided but so many were seeking 'a way'.

Christian revival as well as Indian cults, mysticism and magic were very active as was the devil. Live for today, enjoy life, hedonism in all its worst forms attracted many poor souls.

Remember Sodom, remember Gomorra, they are gone, but look at our inner cities, look to our crime rates, look at the despair that haunts people's lives when they don't know the love of God. Find a woman, live together and have children then when it gets difficult and there is no one to turn to, leave and start the whole cycle again.

I was guilty of doing just that throughout my life until I found salvation.

I am not saying things still won't get difficult or for that matter impossible to bear (violence or adultery is hard to deal with, I know) but with Jesus at your side you will not have to bear it alone and that is such a huge comfort and joy.

But what of all the violence and wrong doing in this world, can we do anything about it, really?

Yes, oh yes, it can all be swept away by love, but it has to be through the love of Jesus. I truly believe that one day it is going to happen. He is returning. These may well be 'the end times' the bible tells of.

But I digress, the 70's. I was serving in the RAF on a unit that had heavy transport aircraft (Hercules).

It was, I remember, a warm sunny day and I was out on the airfield servicing equipment. A chap I vaguely knew drove past and waved on his way to service an aircraft. We had been to a few of the same parties, smoked the odd joint at the weekends but he wasn't a big user, neither was I then, I waved back and on he went.

I was never to see him again.

Later I went back for lunch in the mess. The place was buzzing, people all talking about this guy and what he had done.

It appears he had climbed onto the wing of an aircraft, stood at the edge and dived off onto the concrete 10ft below. Witnesses said it was as if he was going swimming. That's all anyone knew at that time as he was taken direct to hospital with arm neck and head injuries. Word came back after a few days that he had got away with a few bones broken and concussion, and was expected to make a full recovery. I admit on my part I forgot about him after that, as I said I didn't really know him enough to go visiting or follow up on how he was getting on.

His kit was packed up by someone and his room cleaned out. He never came back.

Weeks later we heard a story that he had been court-martialled and dismissed from the RAF. Nothing official just the grapevine working as it does in all big organizations.

It appears that he had been a regular user of LSD at the weekends and on leave.

This had been a 'flashback', a vision so real he had believed he was diving into a swimming pool at his girlfriend's house.

That cost him his career, he was lucky, it could so easily have cost him his life.

I had never used it at this point in my life, after seeing what could happen I never would.

I only mention this because had I been a user of this type of drug I would perhaps have had some misgivings about 'seeing' things or hearing God speaking to me.

What do I mean by God speaking? Do I mean voices in my head, well yes and no? I don't mean I have a conversation and hear the replies, I do mean I hear a voice that is not a thought and is not your own. Some people say they clearly hear a voice, others it's just that 'still small voice' the bible speaks of. All I can say is that this account is from my perspective. I don't claim to be an authority on the subject; I can only recount what happens to me.

It's a feeling, clarity of thought that isn't your own, even a strong impression or need. In short it can be almost anything. If you have faith then, you 'know' it is God 'speaking' to you; it's so different, so clear and obvious that you can't have any doubts. It feels like nothing else.

An example: The first time I ever heard God speak to me and realized it, because this probably wasn't in fact the first time, I just hadn't been listening I was driving to meet with some people I had known for years in the village I used to live in before I was baptised. I wasn't looking forward to it because one of them was a good friend but really anti-God. Not only wouldn't he believe but later he even refused to come to my wedding because it was in a church, as if the building would infect him with Christianity!

He still, even now, resists using my name and will call me by my old name. As for the others, this was a first meeting since my baptism and I didn't know how they were going to react both to the name change and my being saved. And yes I was nervous and a little shy about it, all very English. You may know the feeling, part of you wants to cry out 'I have been saved, praise the Lord' and part of you is saying 'don't do it people will think you are weird'. I wish I had the courage to always cry out in praise of the Lord. I haven't, but I am trying.

As I drove into the village I passed the 'Welcome to' sign, there as clear as if it had been spoken to me I heard these words.

'Even though I walk through the valley of the shadow of death, I will fear no evil, for you are with me;'

Psalm 23 verse 4

These words rang in my head and I knew without any doubts that the Lord God had spoken to me. It wasn't just the words; it was how they sounded, not like my thoughts at all, more like a voice. I have no, repeat no doubts it was Jesus speaking to me.

All in all, things went okay when I met with the friends I was visiting but I didn't worry from the moment I heard His voice. I knew no matter what happened He was with me.

Remember, I was for many years at best a sceptic, so for me to have this happen was an incredible feeling. I KNEW Jesus was with me. Not I felt it, or thought it, it was a fact.

So God does speak to His disciples. That was the first time for me. Since then He has spoken to me many times. Sometimes in church a verse number from the bible will pop into my head, and here it is important that you realise, because of my brush with meningitis, I cannot do what so many do and that is to quote passages from the Bible, 'in Mark 3 verse 7 it says' I can't do it... so when I am given a verse number I usually have no idea what it is, I have to take it on faith as His word. Sometimes I am compelled to take it forward to my pastor and read to all gathered at the meeting.

So you can see it is not a casual thing that happens and must not be treated as such. It is the word of God, given by Him for me or for others.

On one occasion I was giving my testimony in front of the church when everything went into soft focus for a few seconds and all I could do was to look at this one woman sitting near the back with a man next to her. She was the only person in sharp focus.

I was given something to tell her, that small voice again, and then it was over, everything was back as before. What I thought odd at the time is that for me, this had taken at least a few seconds of silence while I looked at her. Nobody else there noticed anything; apparently I had just continued talking without a break. I am trying to be completely straight forward about things in this account but I do realise if you are a non-Christian reading this then some of it might be hard to believe. All I can really say to you is it is the truth about what has really happened to me. Jesus has saved me from sin and now I do not lie. What you are getting here is the truth, believe it or not, it's up to you. One thing to perhaps consider carefully though. Who benefits if you don't believe me? Could it be satan? Please, think about that.

After I had finished speaking I went to the woman I had looked at. Privately, I told her what I had been given for her. She told her partner, the man with her. They both understood and confirmed it made sense to them even though it made no sense to me. I then told my pastor what I had done and why.

I could give you many more examples but this isn't meant to be a diary just an account so we will move on.

Visions:

'Oh dear' I can hear you say, well I can't blame you after all we are talking about seeing things that aren't really there aren't we, or are we?

Every day we watch the television, well I have got news for you, those things you are watching aren't really there, it's just a stream of electrons making a chemical coating glow that our eyes 'see' as a picture. When we talk about watching the wind 'look at that wind blow' what we mean is 'look at the effect the wind is having on the objects we can see' as we can't see the wind.

We see things all the time that aren't there, in our dreams, both sleeping and waking; we see pictures and events occurring. How real is a nightmare to you as you are dreaming it?

Doesn't an artist 'see' a painting or a sculptor 'see' what is to be carved before it is started in the so called 'mind's eye'?

A sculptor once told me that all she did was let the sculpture out of the stone. It was already there fully formed; all she did was to remove the excess stone that was surrounding it.

The point I am trying to make is we 'see' in many different ways. Visions are just another way of 'seeing', a way given by God.

For me there have been maybe five or six times when a vision has been given to me. There may have been more but at first I used to deny them as imagination, now, however I have learned to have faith in the fact that a vision 'looks' and feels very different to imagination. The only way I can put it is to say imagination is a picture of something you are looking at, in a vision you are there, it is reality.

My first - I saw a closed dark room, I was in it, a door was open just a crack with sunlight shining through making a sharp line across the floor and up the opposite wall. I was cold and lonely and not a little afraid. I knew that all I had to do was open the door and walk through to be safe but to do that would take an effort of will on my part; nobody could do it for me.

I was in church and took the vision to my pastor who had me describe it to the church as a whole. One person came forward later and said she had been sitting wanting to give herself to Jesus but was afraid. My vision had clearly told her not to be afraid and to do it but it had to be her choice and by her effort to leave that dark place and come into the light of God's love.

When Kris was in hospital having her knee replacement surgery I was like any husband worried for her.

I had waited with her until she went to theatre and then was sent home by the nurses and told to ring later, they don't like you being underfoot do they!

As I was leaving the hospital I looked for the chapel so I could go somewhere quiet and pray for Kris and ask Jesus to be with her. I didn't find it so I decided to sit in the car park and pray. I found it on a subsequent visit. Sadly it had the look and feel of a spare room. I thought at the time how much more difficult it would be to accept the loss of a loved one in such a room as that. The problem I felt was it was so multi faith it ended up being a place of no faith. In fact an empty room would have felt and been more honest.

I know we don't need anywhere special to talk to Jesus but if a room is set aside for worship or contemplation then I think it should at least have curtains at the windows, and not have a pile of boxes stored in one corner. I continued to pray in my car when I wanted to be alone or with Kris when we were together.

Anyway this is a copy of the e-mail I sent my pastor as soon as I got home after visiting her that first afternoon.

Hi (*name deleted*)

Something I must share with you that can't wait until Sunday.

Kris is fine starting to wake up now, I will be going in to see her tonight (one visitor only). I will let you know how she is doing and when she maybe out as soon as I know. What I wanted to share:

When I had said bye to her in pre op earlier I left the hospital and just sat in the car and prayed that all would be well and that Jesus would be close to her in this time of need, if I say when you pray sometimes it feels as though you have a really close link with God, really close, this was one of those times when I felt he was with me and answering my prayer, I felt disconnected from myself, as though I was no longer 'here' but drifting in a dark but warm friendly safe place, but still aware of the world. I had a vision, clear as if I was there of Jesus standing by the op table holding Kris's hand, she was on her side facing away from me and Jesus was towards me, his right hand was in hers and his left hand was on his chest. he was golden but not glowing or maybe just a little and in a sort of soft focus but at the same time solid and I could see his face as he looked at me, he had a beard, high cheekbones and really deep eyes, he also had a hood partly pulled onto his head and long hair at least to the shoulder showing under it, mid brown and maybe wavy.

A feeling of joy I cannot describe filled me and I knew that Jesus was saying 'I am here already' at that moment I knew Kris was going to be okay and that there was no need for worry all was well.

I am still buzzing from it, I feel so humble that he gave me that vision but at the same time I want to shout from the rooftops MY GOD LIVES!

I can describe the scene I saw in more detail but have nothing really significant to add to the above.

Please get back to me I feel as though I need to talk to you I really don't know why but it is all wrapped up in what has happened.

Phone me if you can I am at home.

God Bless

Chris

As you can see I was pretty shook up by it because it was the most intense, real, vision I have ever had. My pastor got back to me within hours and we talked about the possible meanings of my vision. He helped me to understand it and to accept it.

As I said at the beginning of this chapter:

Not so many years ago if someone had come to me and said "I had a vision, I saw an angel" or 'I saw Jesus' I would have been really impressed and wanted to know what drug they were using, or perhaps thought 'what a nut!'.

Now with what has happened to me I will still be impressed but never doubt again that some visions are real.

I talked to Kris and without telling her why asked her about the position she had been in before the operation began, it was just as I had seen.

It isn't easy after a lifetime of denial to accept these things even though I have no doubts, so I know for some of you reading this it will be even harder. All I can say is I have come to know the truth, and that truth is the Lord my God is real.

Speaking in Tongues

When I first heard someone do this I have to admit I thought 'what on earth is that all about'? Well that's the point isn't it; it's not of this earth it's from God.

Some people seem to speak this heavenly language so fluently others not at all. Some know what they are saying, others not. Some people can 'translate' what another is saying.

Myself, well once or twice I have been heard to sing in tongues, sometimes I have been aware, other times, it has felt like I was just drifting as if asleep. I can't explain it, nor do I want to. I can only tell you this, it feels wonderful.

One of the most beautiful things I have ever heard was when a young lady in church changed from singing in English to singing in tongues. Her voice lifted all the hairs on the back of my neck. A shiver ran through me. Somehow I knew she was praising God, I could almost get the words. I could 'feel' them and understand them but not translate them. I know that doesn't make sense, but it is as close as I can get to explaining the sensation.

One further comment here though, I sing badly, or at least poorly, I often say that I sing in one key and flat! God gave me this voice so He must be happy to listen to it! I have been told that when I sing in tongues it is lovely, not like me singing. However to be fair it is my wife saying that and she is just a little biased! Isn't God wonderful!

Prophecy

Bible prophecy or biblical prophecy is the prediction of future events based on the action, function, or faculty of a prophet. (www.wikipedia.org)

Or,

A message of divine truth revealing God's will.

The act of uttering such a message. (Collins English dictionary)

When you read that it all sounds very simple doesn't it, but who really wants to be a prophet? I know I didn't. Somehow, I don't see myself, hair blowing in the wind waving my staff like some 21st century Elijah (an Old Testament prophet) astride a great rock. Or, worse still, scribbling away in code afraid to allow anyone to read my predictions, as Nostradamus had to.

There is a book in the bible that is devoted to a prophecy delivered through John (a disciple of Jesus) and authored by Jesus the Messiah.

The last book of the bible Revelation

The revelation of Jesus Christ, which God gave him to show to his servants the things that, must soon take place. He made it known by sending his angel to his servant John, who bore witness to the word of God and to the testimony of Jesus Christ, even to all that he saw.

Revelation chapter 1, verses 1-2

So the bible clearly accepts prophecy, but for me it is the hardest of all gifts to accept.

I kept asking myself 'how can any man know the future' but I am then reminded that as far as God is concerned present, past and future are as one. Well if God knows all things, what happens to free will?

This is a question I have struggled with and I don't know if I am happy with my answer even now. But isn't that the joy of faith, to be able to inquire and learn while still believing God's message. Where every time we learn a new fact it reinforces our faith, however long we have struggled to understand.

Eventually we must also accept that some things are known only to God. My answer and I repeat this is my opinion, please take this as intended, an opinion. God knows all we will do and have done. He lets us make our choices, and he is, in this sense, an observer outside time as we understand it. A story recently told to me to illustrate this point.

A father gives his child a bowl of ice-cream and a bowl of Brussel sprouts. He knows that the child hates sprouts and loves ice cream. In a sense he has fore knowledge of the choice his child will make. He 'knows' the child will choose the ice cream. However the child has free will and can choose the sprouts.

God knows the choices we will make. He can look back from the end of our life to this moment or before we make a choice. He is all knowing while we retain free will.

If you want to pursue this further please talk to a Christian minister or pastor.

My reason for all the above is in part to try to explain to myself and I hope to you the reader what I did in June 2011. Below is a copy of a statement I gave to a visitor to my church who had come to preach.

I have never prophesised before or since so why this and why then? I believe the answer is very simple. God used me to give this to the visitor, it was not for me. I was just the tool he used.

He may use me again or He may not, I am His disciple and His servant.

The last time *(name deleted)* visited I had a picture given to me of the world as seen from space with a band of fire running around it consuming all in its path leaving the ground behind scorched and black. The picture was crystal clear and as fresh in my mind as if I were looking at it in person. It troubled me that I had no idea what it meant or who it was for. I told two church elders what I had been given and frankly left it at that other than thinking of it now and again. I felt strongly that it wasn't for me, but I had no idea who it was for. Now *(name deleted)* is back. I came to hear him speak on Saturday and then again on Sunday. It wasn't until we prayed for the young men and women that another vision was given to me, again completely clear, I saw a forest with the underbrush being burnt away, the ground behind it blackened, I used that vision as I prayed, some of the young men may remember being told to go out into the world and burn like a forest fire to remove the old wood and renew the word in the nations as a fire renews the forest. I believe God has shown me the same vision as I originally saw but in a way I can easier understand now as I used to teach horticulture. *(Name deleted)* has been given the task by the church of seeking out men and women who will go out and spread the word, I believe this is a prophecy given for him of his young people burning away the complacency and sin in the world and spreading the word of Jesus like a fire renewing faith across the nations.

Chris 13th June 2011

When I first became a Christian and accepted Christ as my Saviour I was unsure what to do with the gifts I had been given. Were they real? It all seemed so fantastic. In many ways I was scared to be 'open' to God at first, afraid of losing my independence, afraid of being a passenger in my own life. If you are not a Christian then I can never explain how it feels to be in the presence of God, or just why I now have no fear of death.

In the same way I cannot explain how I know that this isn't self-delusion or fakery. You must look at the evidence for yourself and ask, if not God then how?

I really mean it. Ask yourself the questions, look at the evidence. Don't be fooled and led astray by fantasy books or 'new bibles'. You have a brain; don't be a sheep, think for yourself. Only you can make the choice between the salvation of Christ and damnation.

I'm not joking here, that really is the choice you have to make. Remember, <u>doing</u> <u>nothing</u> is a choice. By doing nothing to save yourself you are in fact giving yourself to Satan.

The devil will always be there by your side. It doesn't matter if you believe in him or not, there he is. Only by taking Christ as your savior and repenting your sins can you be saved. Open the door from the dark place and come into the light of God's love.

Nobody was more surprised than me when I was saved. After the life I have led why would He save me? He saved me because He loves all of us without exception and that includes <u>you</u>. If this book has made you think about your life then please don't waste this chance. Come to the Lord, let Him be part of your life, you will never be alone again.

A Married man May 2011

Chapter 6. Proof at Last

So Far

Dear reader, if you have read this far then you now know some of the details of my life.

It's not all here; I have missed out many boring parts as they added nothing to this story. I have left out the years of just living one day after another, living for the day, never mind tomorrow. All those wasted years when I denied God. And of course the many drunken and stoned days and nights when I tried to blot out the life I was living with drugs or alcohol, one after another.

I have also missed some other parts that were just repetition of events already chronicled. Did you really want to read all the details of my childhood abuse? Was I to carefully chronicle each event in all its horror, I hope not. I hope I have given you an honest flavour of both my childhood and my life to this point.

Nothing that is relevant to this account has been intentionally omitted however painful the memory or the telling. I have tried to be completely honest.

What I have tried to do is write an honest account of my life and the experiences and choices that made me who I am today.

Kris prayed for me and helped me get through the difficult times. We prayed together for protection and strength. Without her support I don't know if I would have had the courage to be as honest and open as I have been.

For some of you reading this it will be difficult to believe all I have written here but I ask you this, why would I lie? What have I to gain?

Jesus died on the cross for me to take my sin and give me a new life. As a Christian I have accepted Him as my saviour. I have given Him my life. He knows my heart. When I pass from this life

I firmly believe that I will be with Him. I thank God that I am alive, and that I have come to His love before it was too late for me.

I will never again be one of Satan's disciples. I will now spend my life praising Jesus and serving Him, until; at last, I meet Him.

Death holds no fear for me, because I will go to my saviour. Please don't misunderstand me here, I, just like you don't want to die just yet, but when I do it will be without fear of what comes after.

Listening to people talk about death I have the feeling that they don't really believe it is going to happen to them, trust me, it is. We are all going to be judged. We will all one day stand before our maker.

If you are struggling with Satan, I pray this will help you. It is never too late to turn to the lord. Never too late to change your life and save your soul.

Writing this hasn't been easy. Many times I wanted to stop because of the memories that were being brought up from my past, but I couldn't. If by recounting my mistakes before I was saved helps even one person turn to the Lord, then it has been worth it.

It is my prayer that the pain and suffering of my life both inflicted upon me, and inflicted by me will, by writing this, help others in similar situations come to the love of God.

It is never too late but please don't delay. No man knows the time of his passing or when he will be judged.

Only Jesus can save you. Only He can make you anew, washed clean of your sins and born again.

Where my life will go now I have no idea. Both Kris and I strongly believe God has a purpose for us, that He is going to use us. We thought perhaps in Albania. We feel there is work for us there. We also have a strong feeling for India, so much so that for our wedding presents we asked all our guests to donate to 'i-connect' it is a charity supporting projects in India, such as giving breeding goats to families. We wanted to help in a practical way. Thanks to the generosity of our guests we collected £1,600, praise God.

Recently at a Christian gathering (North) Kris and I had prayed for guidance and help. We were spoken to by God, 'go where you can do the most good'.

By that I mean that during prayer, we had asked God to help us by telling us where we should go to do His work. We both feel very strongly that He does have work for us. That was our answer. So now we will have to wait and see where we are led. At the same time we will seek a place where we are needed. We are not passive in following God's will; we will be actively seeking our place. We know that with God's guidance we will find it.

As I said earlier, I have given my life to Christ, He steers for me now, and I go where He takes me.

No matter where that is I will go without fear and in faith because I know Jesus my saviour and lord will be with me.

How many years ago was it that I argued against the very existence of God? I look back on that life and wonder why couldn't I see, why was I so blind?

My life now is so different to then. Yes I still have problems just like everyone else. Bills need paying, my computer broke down and had to be repaired right in the middle of writing this, okay, yes, I admit it; I didn't back my data up and lost most of the working versions revisions. Not however the original thankfully. All the unforeseen problems of life that test us, I still get grumpy! I am not perfect, neither is my life. I have had a long period of illness this year, and have spent a considerable amount of time off work because of it. The stress of teaching disadvantaged young people was finally getting to me, I was no longer enjoying my work, and in fact I really didn't want to be there anymore. I finally told my line manager that I couldn't come back to the stress levels I had been subjecting myself to. I have now lost my job because of that illness and other factors that as a Christian I was finding I couldn't accept as part of the teaching I had to do. Thankfully I have had help from my doctor and a councillor and friends from church who have helped me to understand the situation I am in more clearly. I am now on another path, as one door closes another opens, more of that later. Nobody else knew, not even my pastor. Kris and I are private people who don't ask for help very often other than from our Lord, this may be a fault but we don't discuss our private life. For me it is about being able to trust and as yet I still find that so very difficult.

I have prayed and will continue to pray for God's help with my problems. I know He will help because He loves me.

With Jesus at my side I feel so different now. Every day is a joy. I open the curtains and no matter what my problems are I look out and marvel at what God has done for all of us. I see the beauty of the earth and the life upon it and the perfection of His work.

So why do I feel like this? So what is different now? To that there is a very simple answer. Jesus is with me now, I am not alone. All my life I felt alone. I spent so much of my life in ignorance of Jesus, and in ignorance of the joy having Him in my life could bring. If only I had known. All my life I had a friend and a Saviour within reach if only I had put out my hand to Him. How different would my life have been?

Kris and I have now been to visit India in our continuing search for where God wants us. Our church helps support a school there. We believe it is our calling to move there. We are paddling, Jesus is steering, and He knows our destination. That is enough. Are we willing to just give up all we have and go where He sends us? Yes we are. No reservations. We will go where we can do the most good. There is useful work for us in India, so much we can give.

We both feel very strongly that we are being sent there, this does not feel like home to us anymore, Kris says she feels as if she is visiting.

We can make a difference to so many and from the moment we arrived it felt as though we had truly come home. We have no doubts that God is directing us, guiding us on the path He has laid out. So we are going, in faith and with the belief that our Lord is sending us.

So, yet another chapter is beginning. A year ago the thought that I would move to India would never have occurred to me, in fact not so many years ago the thought of being married and a Christian and moving to India would have been pure fantasy. Isn't God amazing! What's next? Who knows, Kris and I are off to find out, guided by our Saviour Christ Jesus.

Last word

When I started this account I thought there would be a beginning, middle and an end. I realise now that there will never be an end. So to you, dear reader, I say thank you for reading this and I pray this account does some good in this world, I pray it helps someone.

In answer to that question, 'can a leopard change his spots?' all my life the answer was no. That has changed since my acceptance of Christ as my saviour and my baptism to Yes, but only with God's help and love. Do you want proof? I am the proof!

Finally, I thank You, Jesus, for being with me throughout my writing of this. For giving me the strength to continue when it was difficult for me and, for your love throughout, always at my side now and forever, until at last I sit at the feet of you my saviour, Christ Jesus.

Amen.

Appendix

All biblical references in this account are taken from the 'English Standard Version' of the Bible.
Published by Crossway Bibles Wheaton, Illinois

'The Two World Wars' by Brigadier Peter Young and Susan Everett
Published by W.H.Smith and Son 1982
ISBN 0 86124 059 6

'i-connect' for more details and how to donate
Contact Mark Speller at Emmanuel Church Durham

To contact Emmanuel Church Durham
http://www.emmanuel.org.uk
Tel: 0191 3861077

To contact the author please e-mail
drwatsonsmate@yahoo.com

Cover designs by C Hyde from an original photograph,
by Mr P A Brett.

Original Artwork 'The Child' by Kris 2012

India 2011, another chapter begins.